Cambridge Elements ☰

Elements in Criminology
edited by
David Weisburd
George Mason University
Hebrew University of Jerusalem

TOWARD A CRIMINOLOGY OF TERRORISM

Gary LaFree
University of Maryland

CAMBRIDGE
UNIVERSITY PRESS

Shaftesbury Road, Cambridge CB2 8EA, United Kingdom

One Liberty Plaza, 20th Floor, New York, NY 10006, USA

477 Williamstown Road, Port Melbourne, VIC 3207, Australia

314–321, 3rd Floor, Plot 3, Splendor Forum, Jasola District Centre, New Delhi – 110025, India

103 Penang Road, #05–06/07, Visioncrest Commercial, Singapore 238467

Cambridge University Press is part of Cambridge University Press & Assessment, a department of the University of Cambridge.

We share the University's mission to contribute to society through the pursuit of education, learning and research at the highest international levels of excellence.

www.cambridge.org
Information on this title: www.cambridge.org/9781108986632

DOI: 10.1017/9781108981071

First published 2023

A catalogue record for this publication is available from the British Library.

ISBN 978-1-108-98663-2 Paperback
ISSN 2633-3341 (online)
ISSN 2633-3333 (print)

Cambridge University Press & Assessment has no responsibility for the persistence or accuracy of URLs for external or third-party internet websites referred to in this publication and does not guarantee that any content on such websites is, or will remain, accurate or appropriate.

Toward a Criminology of Terrorism

Elements in Criminology

DOI: 10.1017/9781108981071
First published online: June 2023

Gary LaFree
University of Maryland
Author for correspondence: Gary LaFree, glafree@umd.edu

Abstract: The study of terrorism represents one of the major turning points in criminology of the twenty-first century. In the space of just two decades, research on terrorism and political extremism went from a relatively uncommon niche to a widely recognized criminological specialization. Terrorism research now appears in nearly all mainstream criminology journals; college courses on terrorism and political violence have been added to the curricula of most criminology departments; and a growing number of criminology students are choosing terrorism as a suitable topic for class papers, research topics, theses and dissertations. The purpose of this book is to explore similarities and differences between terrorism and more ordinary forms of crime. This Element considers the ways that criminology has contributed to the study of terrorism and the impact the increasing interest in terrorism has had on criminology. This Element also provides empirical comparisons of terrorist attacks to more ordinary crimes and criminal offenders. This title is also available as Open Access on Cambridge Core.

Keywords: terrorism, radicalization, political extremism, criminology, counterterrorism

ISBNs: 9781108986632 (PB), 9781108981071 (OC)
ISSNs: 2633-3341 (online), 2633-3333 (print)

Contents

1 Introduction   1

2 Impact of Criminology on Terrorism Research and Policy   9

3 Terrorist Attacks, Terrorist Perpetrators and Criminal
   Offenders in the United States   30

4 Worldwide Terrorism and Crime   47

5 Discussion and Conclusions   66

   References   74

1 Introduction

Although research on political extremism and terrorism from criminology scholars began to appear in the 1980s and 1990s (Turk, 1982; Smith, 1994; Hamm, 1998), before the coordinated attacks of September 11, 2001, there was relatively little interest in these topics among criminologists. In fact, at the turn of the twenty-first century it was not at all clear that most criminologists considered terrorism and politically motivated violence to be a legitimate part of criminology. Terrorism was mostly left out of the lexicon of criminology because it did not fit neatly into the model of mainstream criminology. It is not strongly associated with the poorest members of society, its perpetrators rarely see themselves as criminals and most governments do not collect reliable data on how often it occurs.

However, this situation began to change dramatically in the early 2000s. In fact, in a review of the major developments in criminology during the first two decades of the twentieth century, a growing interest in research on terrorism and responses to terrorism would surely qualify as a major turning point. In the space of just twenty years, the study of terrorism and political extremism went from a relatively uncommon niche to a widely recognized criminological specialization. This expansion was no doubt fueled in part by the coordinated attacks of 9/11, but also by a continuing drum beat of high-profile attacks from around the world. A handful of influential examples include the 2002 bombings in Bali; the 2004 Madrid train bombings; the 2005 bombings in London; the 2008 coordinated attacks in Mumbai; the 2011 attacks in Oslo; the 2013 Boston Marathon bombings; the 2015 Beirut bombings; the 2016 bombings in Brussels; the 2017 vehicle ramming attack in Barcelona; the 2019 mass shooting in Christchurch, New Zealand; the 2020 mass shooting in Vienna – and many more. Moreover, while interest in terrorism in the wake of 9/11 was driven mostly by concerns with Islamist extremism, more recently, attention has turned toward domestic threats, especially from right-wing radicals.

Signs of the adoption of terrorism as a major specialty in criminology are everywhere. Terrorism research now appears in nearly all mainstream criminology journals; college courses on terrorism and political violence have been added to the curricula of most criminology and criminal justice departments; and a growing number of criminology students are choosing terrorism and political extremism as suitable topics for class papers, research topics, theses and dissertations. The American Society of Criminology (ASC) has added a Division on Terrorism and Bias Crime that now has as many members as long-standing specializations like organized crime and juvenile delinquency. The European Society of Criminology (ESC) has created a working group on radicalization, extremism and terrorism. And the ASC, the ESC and the

Academy of Criminal Justice Studies now routinely feature dozens of papers and panels on terrorism and counterterrorism each year at their annual meetings.

Defining terrorism has long been a challenge for both researchers and policy makers. The word terrorism starts with the root word "terror" and adds the Greek suffix "ism" to form a noun that can denote a wide variety of behaviors and predispositions, including violent action, adherence to a cause, or belief in specific doctrines or principles. In practice, most research on terrorism either focuses on terrorist attacks or groups, or individuals who support terrorist causes. In this Element, I define terrorist attacks as "the threatened or actual use of illegal force and violence by non-state actors to attain a political, economic, religious, or social goal through fear, coercion or intimidation" (LaFree, Dugan & Miller, 2015: 13). "Threatened" is an important part of this definition because acts like aerial hijacking can be carried out not only by engaging in violence but by threatening to. The reference to "non-state actors" means that I am excluding state-sponsored terrorism. This is an important exclusion. Although valid estimates are hard to come by (Rummel, 1994; McCauley & Moskalenko, 2008), it is likely that far more individuals are killed and injured through state-sponsored terrorism than from the attacks of subnational actors. However, to this point in time, no one has succeeded in obtaining comprehensive data on the terrorist acts committed by states – which is far more challenging than studying individuals and groups engaged in terrorism, many of whom actively seek media attention.

Note that this definition of terrorism applies to actual or threatened terrorist *attacks*. Defining terrorism in terms of the *perpetrators* who carry it out is broader in scope than an inventory of attacks because criminal laws in most countries not only prohibit individuals from committing terrorist attacks but also outlaw individuals from providing material support to terrorist organizations, even if these individuals are not directly involved in attacks. For example, providing funding to a terrorist group or supporting a terrorist organization as an accountant or a driver qualifies as a criminal offense in most countries. To account for individual terrorist perpetrators, I adopt the Federal Bureau of Investigation (FBI; 2017) definition of political extremism as "encouraging, condoning, justifying, or supporting the commission of a violent act to achieve political, ideological, religious, social, or economic goals." Throughout this Element I will refer to terrorists as those who commit or attempt to commit terrorist attacks, and political extremists as those who encourage or support illegal, politically motivated violence.

The integration of terrorism research into the criminological mainstream in the early 2000s marks a major turning point in criminological history. The purpose of this Element is to explore this integration, paying particular attention to similarities and differences between terrorism and more ordinary forms of crime. I will begin by considering the ways that criminology has contributed to the study of terrorism and the impact the increasing interest in terrorism has had on criminology. I will also provide empirical comparisons of terrorist attacks and political extremists to more ordinary crimes and criminal offenders. This Element should be useful to criminologists who have an interest in bringing terrorism into their treatment of crime and to terrorism researchers who have an interest in bringing criminology into their treatment of terrorism and political extremism. In the remainder of this section, I consider how terrorism and responses to terrorism compare with other types of crime. In Section 2, I examine contributions that criminology has made to the study of terrorism. In Section 3, I compare terrorism and other types of crime for the United States, and in Section 4, I do similar comparisons worldwide. In Section 5, I summarize the relationship between criminology and terrorism studies and offer conclusions about the future of this relationship.

Comparing Terrorism to Crime

An appropriate starting point for the argument that terrorism and illegal political extremism should be a part of criminology is provided by Edwin Sutherland, whose famous definition of criminology (Sutherland & Cressey, 1960: 3) includes the "scientific study of making laws, breaking laws, and reacting toward the breaking of laws." Clearly, terrorist attacks as well as behaviors that support terrorist causes involve breaking criminal laws. Moreover, most individuals who are accused of engaging in terrorism are prosecuted under laws prohibiting terrorism-related behavior and then processed by regular criminal justice systems. Clarke and Newman (2006: i) make the connection between criminology and the study of terrorism most directly: "Terrorism is a form of crime in all essential respects." At the outset, we can agree that terrorism represents both the breaking of laws (i.e., criminal behavior) and reactions to the breaking of laws (i.e., criminal justice responses), and as such is a legitimate topic for criminology research. However, given that the term "crime" includes behaviors as diverse as homicide and jaywalking, robbery and polluting navigable waters, it is not surprising that terrorism resembles some forms of crime more than others.

Since its creation in 1929, the Uniform Crime Reports (UCR), collected by the FBI, has provided the major official source of crime data for the United States. The UCR gathers its most extensive data on eight types of crime, referred to as "Part I crimes": murder and nonnegligent manslaughter, forcible rape, robbery, aggravated assault, burglary, larceny, motor vehicle theft and arson (added under a congressional directive in 1979). For comparison purposes, I will consider these eight crimes identified by the UCR as "ordinary" crimes. These crimes are certainly ordinary in the sense that they are common. In 2019, the UCR reported a total of more than eight million Part I crimes (FBI, 2020). Larceny was most frequent, with over five million reported cases. Murder and nonnegligent manslaughter was least frequent, with just over 16,000 cases. In the next two subsections, I consider similarities and differences between terrorist attacks, terrorist perpetrators and more common types of crime and criminal offenders.

Similarities between the Study of Terrorism and the Study of Crime

A basic similarity between terrorism and other types of illegal behavior is clear from Sutherland's already cited definition of criminology (Sutherland & Cressey, 1960: 3): criminology has traditionally been divided into *etiology* (an emphasis on "breaking laws") and *criminal justice* (an emphasis on "making laws" and "reacting toward the breaking of laws"). The same logic can be used to divide the study of terrorism into two major specialties. Studies of how individuals decide to engage in acts that support terrorism can be seen as focusing on the *etiology* of terrorism, while studies examining what legal procedures are best suited to discouraging individuals from engaging in terrorism and reacting to their crimes if these procedures fail can be seen as issues of *counterterrorism* (when the emphasis is on stopping terrorist attacks) or *deradicalization* (when the emphasis is on reforming terrorist perpetrators or those at risk of becoming terrorist perpetrators).

Another important similarity between the study of ordinary crime and terrorism is that both are inherently multidisciplinary; researchers engaged in doing either come from a wide range of academic disciplines. Thus, both criminology research and terrorism studies include contributions from political science, psychology, sociology, economics and anthropology as well as a long list of other fields. This feature has made criminology one of the most interdisciplinary areas of study in the social sciences and offers similar advantage to those studying terrorism. However, at the same time, terrorism studies, like criminology, shares the drawbacks of an intensively multidisciplinary focus. In particular, such a focus complicates communication between researchers, encourages theoretical confusion, and makes it more difficult to develop a shared conceptual framework.

Finally, the study of terrorist perpetrators, like the study of more ordinary criminal offenders, faces the policy challenge of whether to focus on reducing contact between offenders and their subcultures versus reducing criminal behavior. Terrorism researchers make this distinction by contrasting deradicalization and disengagement initiatives. Horgan (2009: 153) defines deradicalization as "the social psychological process whereby an individual's commitment to, and involvement in, violent radicalization is reduced to the extent that they are no longer at risk of involvement and engagement in violent activity" and disengagement as "the process whereby an individual experiences a change in role or function that is usually associated with a reduction of violent participation" (152). Both strategies are based on rehabilitation principles and seek to reduce future terrorist attacks, but they measure success differently. Disengagement strategies categorize a violent extremist who decides to set aside the use of violence for strategic purposes as a success due to the reduction in violence, whereas deradicalization initiatives do not consider these cases a success unless the individual also rejects extremist beliefs (Sumpter, 2017). These challenges are similar to policy approaches to criminal gangs in terms of whether the emphasis should be on reducing gang involvement or disengaging gang members from violence (Decker, Pyrooz & Moule, 2014).

Differences between the Study of Terrorism and the Study of Crime

Having listed several similarities, I identify five important differences between the study of terrorism and the study of more common types of crime.

Terrorist Perpetrators, Unlike Common Criminals, Do Not See Themselves as Criminal

First, although common criminals vary widely in terms of how they perceive their activities (cf., Katz, 1988; Black, 1998; Anderson, 1999), it is safe to say that few criminals see themselves as altruists. By contrast, many terrorist perpetrators see themselves not as criminals but as individuals making sacrifices for a noble cause (Pedahzur, Perliger & Weinberg, 2003; Hafez, 2006). Indeed, many members of the most prominent terrorist groups in the world – including the Islamic State, al Qaeda, Shining Path, Euskadi ta Askatasuna or Basque Homeland and Freedom (ETA), the Irish Republican Army (IRA), the LTTE and the FARC – often conceive of themselves as freedom fighters and positive agents of change.

Lack of Traditional Criminology Data on Terrorism

Second, although data on crime are far from perfect, criminologists have traditionally had three major options for studying criminal behavior, corresponding to the major social roles connected to criminal events: "official" data collected by legal agents, especially the police; "victimization" survey data collected from the general population, which include both crime victims and nonvictims; and "self-report" survey data collected from offenders. However, all three of these sources are problematic when it comes to gathering data on terrorism (LaFree & Dugan, 2004). Few countries develop systematic data on terrorism-related crimes and certainly no worldwide official police data on terrorism exists. Indeed, thus far, the United Nations (UN) has been unable to provide a definition of terrorism that is accepted by all member nations. Police departments in most countries do not maintain separate records for terrorism-related offenses, and much primary data collected by intelligence agents are not available to researchers working in an unclassified environment. Nor are data collection challenges confined to the police. Most individuals convicted of behavior that would be widely regarded as terrorism do not show up in court records as terrorist perpetrators because they are convicted not of terrorism but of more common crimes connected to terrorist behavior, like weapons violations and homicide.

Official data on terrorism in the United States provides an example. The UCR does not include statistics on terrorist attacks. Following the passage of a National Defense Authorization Act, starting in 2015, the FBI (in cooperation with the Department of Homeland Security and the Director of National Intelligence) began reporting data on domestic terrorism (FBI, 2021). The annual report also includes intelligence assessments, a discussion of investigative activities and a list of recommendations. However, this reporting system is limited to arrests, uses a different methodology than the UCR data collection for ordinary offenses and is not integrated with the UCR system.

Starting in 1973, each year the National Crime Victimization Survey (NCVS), administered by the US Census Bureau, has interviewed approximately 240,000 persons in 150,000 households about their experience as crime victims, including assault, burglary, larceny, motor vehicle theft, rape and robbery (Bureau of Justice Statistics, 2022). However, victimization surveys have been of little use in providing statistical evidence on the characteristics of terrorist attacks or its perpetrators. Despite the attention it gets in the media, terrorist attacks are much less common than more ordinary types of violent crime and thus, even with extremely large sample sizes, few individuals in most countries will have been victimized by terrorists. Indeed, victims of terrorism often have no direct contact with perpetrators (e.g., in many bombings), and in too many cases, terrorism victims are killed by their attackers, leaving no one to survey.

A final option for crime data in general is the self-report survey, where individuals are asked to describe their participation in past criminal behavior (Hindelang, Hirschi & Weis, 1979). Self-report surveys in criminology have been especially useful for either studying minor crimes or reporting on criminal behavior when respondents were juveniles (Huizinga & Elliott, 1986; Farrington, Ohlin & Wilson, 1998). Self-report surveys based on interviews with current or former terrorist perpetrators have also provided some excellent scholarship (McCauley, 2002; Horgan, 2004). However, most active terrorists are unwilling to participate in interviews, and even when they are willing, doing interviews with them raises obvious challenges. Terrorism researcher Ariel Merari (1991: 90) described the problem succinctly: "The clandestine nature of terrorist organizations and the ways and means by which intelligence can be obtained will rarely enable data collection which meets commonly accepted academic standards." Hence, self-report surveys have been of little use in providing national let alone worldwide statistics on terrorist attacks or the characteristics of perpetrators.

Common Crimes Are Usually Local; Terrorism Often National or International

Third, for most ordinary crimes, criminal justice decisions are made locally and rarely gather international or even national attention. By contrast, terrorist attacks are frequently reported outside of the local area where they occur and often gather worldwide coverage. For example, incidents like the January 2015 attack on the satirical newspaper *Charlie Hebdo* in Paris, or the April 2013 attack on the finish line of the Boston Marathon create enormous media attention. A Google search of the latter while this Element was being prepared yielded sixty-four million hits. However, this distinction does not mean that terrorist perpetrators are always unmindful of local targets. For example, as we shall see later, there is evidence that terrorist perpetrators, like ordinary offenders, often choose targets in familiar locations (Hasisi et al. 2020b).

Common Criminals Seek Anonymity; Terrorist Perpetrators Seek Media Attention

Fourth, although ordinary criminals are usually struggling to avoid detection much less an audience, a large audience is precisely what many terrorist perpetrators are seeking. A half-century ago, terrorism researcher Brian Jenkins noted that (1975: 15), "terrorists want a lot of people watching and a lot of people listening, and not a lot of people dead." Hoffman (1998: 131) argues that terrorist groups seek maximum publicity for their actions, and because of this fact, getting picked up by the print, and increasingly, the electronic media, is critical to their perceived success. Because a common goal of terrorism is to gain media attention, terrorist attacks are often carefully orchestrated. This is much less common with ordinary crimes.

Terrorism, Unlike Common Crime, Is Often a Means to Broader Goals

Finally, the goal of most ordinary crimes is to obtain a particular material reward, such as money or valued goods, or to kill or injure a specific victim. By contrast, the overriding objective of terrorism and its ultimate justification is to further a political cause. Thus, criminals often have selfish, personal motives, and their actions are not intended to have consequences or create psychological or political repercussions beyond the criminal act. By contrast, the fundamental aim of terrorist perpetrators is often to overthrow or change the dominant political system. Terrorism expert Martha Crenshaw (1983: 2) points out that "the intent of terrorist violence is psychological and symbolic, not material." This conclusion was well supported in a recent study with my colleagues (Becker et al., 2022) in which we examined forty-five US gang members and thirty-eight US political extremists. Compared to gang members, extremists were far more likely to be motivated by the perceived moral authority of their actions. By contrast, we found that gang members were more likely to cite material rewards or group prestige as their main motive for criminal involvement. At the same time, it is clear that the motives of political extremists are not universally nonmaterial. For example, in a study of suicide bombers, Perry and Hasisi (2015) find that perpetrators frequently consider self-gratifying benefits in making the decision to launch attacks.

Conclusions

Much of the confusion about whether political extremism and terrorism are suitable concerns for criminology research comes from the fact that these topics do not fit neatly into mainstream criminology. Terrorism and violent political extremism clearly qualify as criminal, and they also share several important characteristics with more ordinary crime, including the natural division between criminal etiology and law enforcement, an interdisciplinary emphasis and a tension between isolating offenders from criminal subcultures versus stopping or curtailing their offending. However, differences are also apparent and include the fact that terrorist perpetrators, unlike more common criminal offenders, typically do not see themselves as criminals, are often seeking media attention and typically view their actions as furthering broader goals. Moreover, the study of terrorism lacks the main sources of traditional data that are available in criminology, and unlike most common crimes, terrorism frequently has national or even international implications. In the next section, I consider some of the ways that criminology has influenced research on the causes and consequences of terrorism.

2 Impact of Criminology on Terrorism Research and Policy

As terrorism began to gather more policy and research attention in the early 2000s, it made sense to look for theoretical guidance and methodological tools from social and behavioral science disciplines that seemed relevant for understanding the causes and consequences of terrorism, but were more established than the field of terrorism studies. In the first part of this section, I consider how researchers interested in terrorism began to tap criminology theories for help in understanding terrorism. In the next part of the section, I explore how the application of research methods commonly used in criminology have been applied to terrorism. And finally, I consider some of the advantages of responding to terrorism using traditional criminal justice systems.

Theoretical Contributions

A common criticism of early terrorism research was that it lacked a theoretical framework that would help researchers interpret empirical findings (Borum, 2017; Freilich & LaFree, 2015). In looking over the recent criminology literature on terrorism and political extremism, we can conclude that while it has been a relatively slow process, researchers have begun to apply theoretical perspectives from criminology to help understand terrorism and responses to terrorism. In a recent review with my colleague Yesenia Yanez (LaFree & Yanez, In press), we identified a set of twelve refereed criminology journals that publish high-quality empirically based research.[1] We looked for all articles in these journals from 2000 to 2020 that contained the terms "radicalization," "extremism" or "terrorism." We excluded articles that focused only on hate crimes, nonideologically motivated mass shootings or genocide. I summarize our findings in Table 1.

Our review of criminology journals over the past twenty-one years yielded 107 terrorism-/extremism-related articles, suggesting that research on radicalization, political extremism and terrorism now represents a major subfield within criminology. Moreover, we found evidence that the pace at which researchers interested in terrorism are adopting criminological perspectives is accelerating over time. As shown in Table 1, nearly four-fifths of the terrorism research articles applying criminological theories appeared after 2010. Our review also suggests that criminology research on terrorism has often lacked theoretical grounding. Thus, Table 1 shows that nearly half of the articles we

---

[1] The journals reviewed were *Annual Review of Criminology, British Journal of Criminology, Criminology, Criminology and Public Policy, European Journal of Crime and Justice, Journal of Criminal Law and Criminology, Journal of Criminology, Journal of Experimental Criminology, Journal of Quantitative Criminology, Journal of Research in Crime and Delinquency, Justice Quarterly* and *Law and Human Behavior*.

Criminology

Table 1 Criminological theories used for research on terrorism in twelve journals, 2000–20

Theoretical perspective	N	% N	N since 2010	% since 2010
Situational/routine activities	20	19	19	95
Rational choice/deterrence	10	9	8	80
Anomie/strain	4	4	4	10
Criminal subcultures	4	4	2	50
Life course	4	4	4	100
Differential association/ learning	3	3	3	100
Social control	2	2	2	100
Social disorganization	2	2	2	100
Collective action theory	1	1	1	100
Conflict/radical	1	1	1	100
Psychological	1	1	1	100
Situational action	1	1	1	100
Social construction	1	1	1	100
Symbolic interaction	1	1	1	100
Atheoretical analysis and reviews	52	49	35	67
Total	107	100	85	79

identified in these leading criminology journals were atheoretical – that is, focused on various aspects of terrorism or counterterrorism that did not include a specific theoretical framework.

Excluding the atheoretical articles, we found fifty-five articles (51.4 percent) that advanced at least one criminological theory. For the articles that were grounded in a specific theory, the most common were situational/routine activities followed by rational choice/deterrence perspectives. Following at some distance were criminal subcultures, life-course approaches, anomie/strain and differential association/ learning. Many influential criminology theories were uncommon (e.g., social control, symbolic interaction) or altogether absent (e.g., labeling, biological). Among the atheoretical articles, the most common topics (in order) were policy arguments, empirical examinations of specific aspects of radicalization, extremism or terrorism (e.g., lone-wolf attacks, female perpetrators), literature reviews and articles about the criminal justice processing of terrorist/extremist cases. I consider in more detail each of the theoretical categories we identified in the next several sections.

Situational Criminology and the Routine Activities Theory

According to Table 1, the most common theoretical perspective in terms of the total times it appeared in the articles we reviewed was situational/routine activities theory. While some criminological theories focus on individual-level variables that contribute to radicalization, a situational approach shifts the attention away from the offender and onto the crime itself (Clarke, 1980; 1995). Routine activities theory is a situational approach that focuses on both the situational determinants (i.e., the suitability of targets and the strength of guardianship) as well as the motivation of criminal offenders (Cohen & Felson, 1979). However, most of the applications of situational perspectives to terrorist perpetrators, like much of the research on crime in general, has emphasized situational determinants more than the motivation of offenders. For example, recent criminology articles that have relied on situational or routine activities perspectives to understand terrorism include studies of terrorist attack "hot spots" (Hasisi, Carmel & Wolfowicz, 2020a), terrorist target characteristics (Sturup, Gerell & Rostami, 2020) and situational crime prevention (SCP) applied to terrorist attacks (e.g., Perry et al., 2017).

In support of earlier studies of common crimes (Sherman, Gartin & Buerger, 1989), Perry (2020) found that a large proportion of the total number of terrorist attacks in the city of Jerusalem were concentrated in a relatively small number of geographic spaces: one-quarter of all attacks occurred in less than 2 percent of all attack locations. This finding has important policy implications as it suggests that terrorism, like more ordinary crimes, does not occur randomly but rather is highly concentrated in relatively well-defined spaces. This insight raises the possibility that societies can deploy police and other preventative measures more effectively to reduce the number of successful terrorist attacks.

Closely related to the situational concept of hot spots, is the idea of "near repeats" – the finding that once criminal offenders select a particular time and place for a crime, if successful, they are likely to continue offending at the same or nearby locations (Townsley, Homel & Chaseling, 2003; Bowers & Johnson, 2004). Building on the possibility that terrorist attacks will also follow near-repeat patterns, Behlendorf, LaFree and Legault (2012) propose a method for identifying and analyzing what they identify as *violent microcycles*; groups of events that take place close to each other in both space and time. They use the Global Terrorism Database (GTD) to analyze 3,335 terrorist attacks attributed to the Farabundo Martí National Liberation Front (FMLN) in El Salvador and 1,993 terrorist attacks attributed to ETA in Spain – two terrorist organizations that were both extremely active and violent but differed greatly in terms of history, grievances and motives. They find strong support for the conclusion that many of the terrorist attacks attributed to these two distinctive groups were part of violent microcycles and that the spatiotemporal attack patterns of these two groups exhibit substantial similarities. Their analysis shows that for both the FMLN and ETA, compared to other tactics used by terrorists, bombings and nonlethal attacks were more likely to be part of microcycles, and that compared to attacks that occurred elsewhere, attacks aimed at national or provincial capitals or areas of specific strategic interest to the terrorist organization were more likely to be part of microcycles.

Closely linked to the situational approach, Cohen and Felson's (1979) routine activity theory suggests that crime occurs when suitable targets, motivated offenders and the absence of capable guardians converge in time and space. Several recent terrorism studies have focused on soft and hard target character-istics along with security-related variables. For example, Fahey et al. (2012) examined whether terrorist hijackings situationally differed from nonideologi-cally motivated aerial hijackings. By examining contextual variables including number of hijackers, day of the week and departure country, the authors found that measures of organizational resources (e.g., number of hijackings, weapon type) differed significantly between terrorist and nonterrorist perpetrators. By focusing on situational characteristics like these, the researchers were able to offer situation-specific policy recommendations.

Clarke (1980) proposed SCP as a method for reducing crime through man-agerial and environmental changes. Situational crime prevention rests on the assumption that offenses, regardless of whether they are carefully planned, are heavily influenced by situational opportunities (Clarke, 1997, 2016). The goal of SCP is to manipulate the environment in order to raise the costs and reduce the benefits of crimes. Clarke and Homel (1997) offer sixteen crime opportun-ity-reducing techniques (e.g., target hardening, natural surveillance). These strategies can also be applied to the prevention of terrorist attacks. For example, based on a situational perspective, Perry et al. (2017) conclude that the "West Bank barrier" in Jerusalem has been effective in preventing suicide bombings.

Rational Choice and Deterrence

According to Table 1, the second most common criminology perspective applied to terrorism research in the major criminology journals reviewed is rational choice or deterrence theory. Clarke and Cornish's (1985) rational choice theory borrows from economics, psychology and sociology to model offenders' decision-making processes. In criminology, this perspective is used primarily to predict an individual's initial involvement in crime. Because rational choice theory assumes that all individuals are decision makers who take incentives and risks into account, deterrence is often the focus of those who apply a rational choice perspective. In research on terrorism, criminologists have used rational choice perspectives most frequently to examine the deterrent effects of various counterterrorism policy initiatives.

The rational choice perspective is especially interesting in the study of terrorism because, as we discussed in the previous section, compared to ordinary criminal offenders, terrorist perpetrators are more likely to perceive the benefits of their crimes in terms of political, ethical or moral gains. Terrorism perpetrators may thus be more likely to engage in political extremism if they perceive the rewards of their actions as outweighing the risks or costs for a particular social cause or political movement. Much of the research in this area tries to gauge the extent to which various deterrent measures implemented by governments are successful either at preventing attacks in general or at preventing attacks on specific target types.

Based on a rational choice perspective, Dugan, LaFree and Piquero (2005) examined aerial hijackings and found that some measures of target hardening like metal detectors and law enforcement at passenger check points significantly reduced the rate of new hijacking attempts. However, the authors also found that these methods were generally limited to nonterrorist hijackers. Likewise, Carson, Dugan and Yang (2020) apply rational choice theory to study the impact of government actions on radical eco-movement attacks and find that when government policies increase the costs of committing this type of extremist behavior, incidents decline.

While most applications of rational choice/deterrence perspectives in criminology have examined whether the threat or imposition of punishment reduces future criminal behavior, the perspective applies equally well to asking whether the threat of punishment instead increases future criminal behavior. Several applications of rational choice/deterrence perspectives in criminology studies of terrorism have looked for possible *backlash* effects of punishment or the threat of punishment. For example, LaFree, Dugan and Korte (2009) compare deterrence and backlash outcomes by examining rates of terrorist attacks in Northern Ireland between 1969 and 1992 as the British imposed various types of counterterrorism interventions. In support of backlash interpretations, the authors discovered that three of the six counterterrorist interventions used by the British during this period significantly increased the hazard of future terrorist strikes, two interventions had no significant effect in either direction, and only one found a short-lived deterrence effect. Similarly, Hsu and McDowall (2020) found that repressive counterterrorism actions increased violence in Israel, and that backlash effects were dependent on the magnitude of government repression, the target and the lethality of terrorist attacks.

Other Criminological Theories

According to Table 1, other criminological theories were less commonly applied in recent terrorism research. Still, there were examples of most mainstream criminology theories, including four studies based on anomie/strain, criminal subcultures and life-course perspectives, three based on differential association/learning perspectives, and two each based on social control and social disorganization perspectives. Thus far, support for anomie/strain theory with regard to terrorist perpetrators is relatively weak, with one article finding that collective strain does not have a direct effect on violent extremist attitudes (Nivette, Eisner & Ribeaud, 2017); one finding an opposite effect (i.e., economically deprived counties were less likely to have far-right perpetrators; Freilich et al., 2015); and another finding effects of collective deprivation only for far-left terrorist attacks (Varaine, 2020).

Three of the four criminological studies that have applied criminal subculture approaches to the study of terrorism have used the perspective to better understand radicalization in prison. While Useem and Clayton (2009) conclude that there are low or modest levels of radicalization in prison, Hamm (2009) and LaFree, Jiang and Porter (2020) find that spending time in prison and being exposed to radicalization in prison increases the likelihood of violent political extremism after release. In the fourth study in this group, Cottee (2020) finds support for a criminal subculture perspective in a study of Western Islamists. He argues that a radical Islamist subculture is composed of three characteristics that heighten the likelihood of extremist behavior: (1) violence and machismo; (2) death and martyrdom; and (3) disdain for the temporal world and its earthly concerns and possessions.

Among the life-course applications, Simi, Sporer and Bubolz (2016) use in-depth interviews with former violent extremists to determine how childhood- and adolescent-related variables influence later patterns of radicalization and violent political extremism. They argue for a three-stage risk-factor model such that the individual: (1) experiences different types of adversity in childhood; (2) subsequently has conduct problems in adolescence; and (3) is then motivated to seek out circumstances that lead to participation in extremist groups. While Simi, Sporer and Bubolz focus on psychological processes leading to radicalization, Carlsson et al. (2020) instead emphasize the social processes that lead to terrorism and political extremism. The authors argue that the process of radicalization occurs in three stages: (1) a weakening of informal social controls; (2) association with individuals close to extremist groups; and (3) a process of "meaning-making" in relation to the group.

Life-course theories have also been used to explain terrorism-related recidivism and desistance. Hasisi et al. (2020a) study offending patterns of imprisoned terrorists and show that many of the risk factors for recidivism are the same for terrorist perpetrators and other types of criminal offenders (e.g., age, prior criminal record). While the life-course perspective typically follows individuals, Miller (2012) examines activities of more than 500 terrorist groups and finds that terrorist organizations that arise more rapidly and attack more frequently also survive longer.

After the original formulation of Sutherland (Sutherland & Cressey, 1960), differential association begins with the premise that criminal behavior, like other behavior, is learned. Specifically, individuals interact in small intimate groups to learn and adopt values that are favorable to breaking the law. By this logic, social learning sometimes overlaps with criminal subcultures. LaFree et al. (2020) argue that imprisonment and prison radicalization increase the probability of post-prison violent extremism because inmates, through association with peers in prison, learn and adopt radical values. This argument is also supported outside of prison as individuals with radical peers are more likely to engage in violent political acts (LaFree et al., 2018). Further, some scholars argue that learning does not necessarily come from associations with deviant peers but can be facilitated by previous high-profile examples. Thus, Miller and Hayward (2019) apply learning theory to understand the contagion-like nature of terrorist attacks where perpetrators purposely ram vehicles into groups of individuals with the intent of killing and injuring as many as possible.

Proponents of the social control perspective argue that crime occurs when an individual's bonds with prosocial communities or institutions are weakened (Hirschi, 1969). Common prosocial bonds include employment, education, marriage and military experience. LaFree et al. (2018) apply this perspective to a sample of American political extremists and find that one variable associated with social control theory (lack of stable employment) is a significant predictor of violent political extremism. Further, in a model that connects social control and strain theories to political aggression, Pauwels, Ljujic and de Buck (2020) find that social integration, or an accumulation of social bonds, increases perceived respect for others and commitment to procedural justice.

In their classic formulation of social disorganization theory, Shaw and McKay (1942) argue that when communities are unable to develop strong social bonds, individuals in those communities will be more likely to engage in a variety of antisocial behavior including crime. This perspective suggests that crime will be more common in areas that lack shared norms and have high population heterogeneity, residential mobility and concentrated disadvantage (Bursik, 1988). LaFree and Bersani (2014) apply the social disorganization perspective to terrorist attacks in the United States and find that counties with high population heterogeneity and residential instability experience high rates of terrorist attacks. The authors also find that counties with high concentrated levels of poverty are associated with few attacks. However, in a more general attempt to explore the applicability of various macro-level theories for understanding terrorist attacks, Freilich et al. (2015) find little support for measures commonly associated with social disorganization theory.

According to Table 1, five articles in our review looked at theoretical perspectives that appeared only once. Four of these articles (Mythen & Walklate, 2006; Arrigo, 2010; Ruggiero, 2010; Ilan & Sandberg, 2019) take a critical look at mainstream criminology theories and encourage researchers to move beyond traditional criminology theories for understanding radicalization and political violence. Three of these articles appeared in the *British Journal of Criminology* and the other appeared in the *European Journal of Criminology*. All four articles recommend some version of a conflict/constructionist perspective as an alternative to a more traditional criminological framework. We classify the fifth article with only a single theoretical mention as psychological. Corner and Gill (2020) analyze ninety case studies to examine the onset of psychological distress across three stages of terrorist involvement (engagement, disengagement and post-disengagement). The authors demonstrate that the relationship between terrorist engagement and psychological distress is mediated by several variables and combinations of variables.

Conclusions: Theoretical Contributions

In general, research on terrorism guided by mainstream criminological theories and published in criminology outlets is still relatively uncommon but clearly growing since 9/11. Based on a review of articles on terrorism and political extremism in twelve leading criminology journals from 2000 to 2020 (LaFree & Yanez, In Press), forty-nine of fifty-four articles (91 percent) that applied a criminological theory to the study of terrorism or political extremism were published after 2010. In other words, the use of criminology theories to explain terrorism and political violence has increased rapidly in the decade since 2010. Nevertheless, mainstream criminology theories like social learning, social control and social disorganization are still rarely applied to understand the etiology of terrorism.

It is important to acknowledge that although the twelve journals reviewed here are among the most influential in the field of criminology, the selection is far from complete. In particular, the journals reviewed exclude articles by criminologists in general social science journals (e.g., *American Sociological Review, Social Forces*) or journals that specialize in the study of terrorism (e.g., *Terrorism and Political Violence, Studies in Conflict and Terrorism*).

The list reviewed also excludes more specialized criminology journals (e.g., *Homicide Studies, Journal of Interpersonal Violence*) and most journals connected to specific countries (e.g., *Australian and New Zealand Journal of Criminology, Canadian Journal of Criminology and Criminal Justice*). In addition, the focus is only on articles published in refereed journals and excludes contributions from monographs and book chapters.

Researchers generally agree that among the purposes of science, description is the most basic. For example, fields like biology began by simply describing flora and fauna. As a field matures, its practitioners are likely to develop increasingly complex scientific methods that move beyond description to explanation, prediction and control. Many of the atheoretical criminology articles reviewed here were efforts to describe specific aspects of extremism, terrorism or the radicalization process. Recent articles, which more often incorporate theoretical perspectives, are also more likely to move beyond description.

The mix of theories represented in the articles reviewed is also of interest. The most common theoretical perspectives that we identified were situational/ routine activities and rational choice/deterrence perspectives. By contrast, we found relatively few articles applying popular mainstream criminology theories like social control, strain and learning. These patterns may tell us something about the current state of data on terrorism and political extremism; in particular, the strong reliance on open source data. In the context of terrorism research, *open source data* are unclassified data drawn from public resources, typically the print and electronic media. As noted earlier, because most common criminological data sources – official police data and victim or offender surveys – are generally not available in the case of political extremism, terrorism researchers have relied extensively on open source data. The fact that nearly all of the theoretical studies we report in this section are based on open source terrorism/ extremism-related data has important implications for the theories being tested and the timing of those tests.

In general, open source terrorism data lend themself to situational/routine activities and rational choice/deterrence perspectives. Given that much of the open source data on terrorism includes information on the characteristics of terrorist attacks (LaFree, 2022), these data usually include information about the situations under which attacks occur (e.g., location, degree of urbanization, time of day). This makes situational perspectives an obvious theoretical choice. Likewise, because much of the open source data being examined focuses on terrorist attacks, it is relatively straightforward to test rational choice/deterrence models by looking at what happens to the rate of terrorist attacks before and after some specific intervention. By contrast, open source event data are often less useful for understanding individual-level decision making. Terrorism event databases like the GTD only include individual information to the extent that it is explicitly linked to attacks (e.g., there were two perpetrators of a mass shooting). Many of the mainstream criminology theories that are underrepresented in our survey of terrorism-related articles (e.g., social control, differential association, situational action theory) require detailed information on the characteristics and behaviors of perpetrators – data that thus far have been less common for those who engage in terrorism.

These considerations may also help explain the timing of theoretical contributions to the literature on political extremism and terrorism. The only three theories that were present before 2010 in the articles reviewed in Table 1 were situational, rational choice and criminal subcultures. Because some open source event databases have been available for decades (Mickolus, 1976; LaFree, Dugan & Miller, 2015), situational and rational choice perspectives were easier to apply before 2010. Further, the two studies grounded in a criminal subcultures perspective and published before 2010 (Useem & Clayton, 2009; Hamm, 2009) were both based on separate data collection projects on political extremists in prison and did not depend on perpetrator databases.

The open source data situation has changed considerably in recent years as new individual-level databases on political extremism have started to appear. Three of the most extensive of these are from the United States: (1) the American Terrorism Study (Smith & Damphousse, 2007); (2) Profiles of Individual Radicalization in the United States (PIRUS; LaFree et al., 2018); and (3) the Extremist Crime Database (Freilich et al., 2014). Two additional individual-level databases focus on Islamist cases in Europe and the United States (Western Jihadism Project; Klausen, Morrill & Libretti, 2016) and on lone actor perpetrators in the United Kingdom and the United States (Lone Actor Terrorist Database; Gill, Horgan & Deckert, 2014). The availability of these databases makes it increasingly feasible to test criminological theories at the individual level, including life course (Hasisi, Carmel & Wolfowicz, 2020a), strain (Varaine, 2020), differential association (LaFree, Jiang & Porter, 2020) and social control (LaFree et al., 2018) perspectives. As more individual-level databases become available in the future, we are likely to see a growing number of articles based on criminological theories that have to this point been relatively uncommon.

The increasing interest in individual-level data on terrorism itself likely represents a shift in research away from explaining crime events (i.e., terrorist attacks) toward understanding criminal development (i.e., radicalization). As 9/11 and the threat of radical Islamist attacks recedes and concerns about domestic, especially right-wing, terrorism increases, there appears to be growing interest in understanding radicalization. In general, individual-level theories like social control and situational action theory may be more relevant than rational choice and situational perspectives for explaining pathways to radicalization.

It is clear that criminological interest in terrorism has grown dramatically since the turn of the twenty-first century. Although there are indications that this specialization within criminology has been undertheorized, I also find evidence that applications of criminological theories to understand terrorism are becoming more common over time. A major challenge in terms of applying criminological theories to radicalization and political extremism is that the nature of terrorism makes it difficult to track individual perpetrators through traditional criminological data sources such as police files or victimization or self-report surveys. In response to this challenge, terrorism researchers have turned to open source data that most often counts terrorist attacks, rather than the characteristics and behaviors of perpetrators. As a result, popular criminology theories that focus on predicting individual offender behavior have been less useful than theories that emphasize where terrorism occurs (e.g., situational/routine activities) and whether it increases or decreases following counterterrorism interventions (rational choice/deterrence). Scholars will likely find it easier to do theoretically driven research in the future as more individual-level data become available.

Methodological Contributions

Research on terrorism and political extremism is frequently criticized for a lack of careful empirical analysis and statistical sophistication (Ranstorp, 2007; Sageman, 2014). In an early review, Schmid and Jongman (1988: 177) identified more than 6,000 published works on terrorism but concluded that most of the research reviewed was "impressionistic, superficial and offers . . . far reaching generalizations on the basis of episodal evidence." Psychologist Andrew Silke (2001: 221) put it more colorfully: "Ultimately, terrorism research . . . . exists on a diet of fast food research: quick, cheap, ready-to-hand and nutritionally dubious." However, as with the application of criminological theories to terrorism, this situation has been rapidly changing. In 2012, the *Journal of Quantitative Criminology* released a special volume on "Quantitative Approaches to the Study of Terrorism" in which contributors highlighted the methodological innovations that were taking place in the area of criminology-oriented terrorism studies. In an editorial introduction, Josh Freilich and I (LaFree & Freilich, 2012) pointed out that until then very few empirical studies of terrorism relied on inferential statistics or testing hypotheses with appropriate controls and accepted statistical methods. However, we also concluded that the amount of methodological sophistication appearing in criminological studies of terrorism was rapidly increasing.

There is evidence that the use of criminological methods to study terrorism has further accelerated in the years since the earlier special issue was published. For example, Schuurman (2020) examined articles published between 2007 and 2016 in nine leading journals that include research on terrorism – many of them done by criminologists. Based on a sample of nearly 3,500 articles, he concludes that the use of more sophisticated data collection and analytic methods has become far more common during this ten-year period, even though it is still the case that only a minority of published papers employ inferential statistics. He also points out that many scholars continue to work alone and that many authors applying novel methods to terrorism research are one-time contributors.

In reviewing research on terrorism over the past few decades, several methods that either originated in criminology or were popularized in criminology have been especially influential for the study of terrorism. These include series hazard modeling, group-based trajectory analysis (GBTA), self-exciting point (SEP) process methods, analysis of spatial and temporal clustering, network analysis, agent-based modeling (ABM) and meta-analysis. I briefly consider recent developments in each of these areas.

Series Hazard Modeling

According to Dugan (2011), the series hazard model is an extension of the Cox (1972) proportional hazard model, and is used to estimate the impact of policy interventions on the risk of additional incidents (in this case, terrorist attacks) controlling for a set of relevant variables. The key distinction between the series hazard model and the more traditional Cox proportional hazard model is that the latter estimates the contributions of covariates to the hazard of repeated events (e.g., terrorist attacks) for one unit rather than for a single event (e.g., arrest) across multiple units. This method is most often used as an alternative to time-series analysis, which also estimates the effects of covariates on outcomes for a single unit over time. Dugan (2011) notes that a major advantage of the series hazard model over standard time-series analysis is the ability of hazard models to capture variation in the timing between events. By contrast, time-series analysis is arbitrary with respect to time in the sense that it aggregates all events to a single time unit (e.g., month, quarter, year) and then counts their frequency.

In the previous section, I mentioned a study by Dugan, LaFree and Piquero (2005) on aerial hijackings in which we used the series hazard model to estimate the deterrent effects of several policies on the hazard of six categories of aerial hijacking, 1931–2003: (1) US hijackings; (2) non-US hijackings; (3) Cuban hijackings; (4) terrorist-motivated hijackings; (5) non-terrorist-motivated hijackings; and (6) all hijackings. The results showed that policies that targeted specific categories of hijackings were most effective – for example, raising criminal penalties in Cuba for Cuba-bound hijackings. However, the results also showed that traditional deterrence strategies like tighter screening methods were ineffective in reducing terrorist-motivated attacks.

A series hazard model was also used in the LaFree, Dugan and Korte (2009) evaluation of six interventions by the British government on IRA terrorist attacks discussed earlier. We found that three of the interventions led to increases in subsequent attacks, two had no impact and only one (a large military operation) was linked to declines in future terrorist attacks. Carson's (2014) use of series hazard models to assess the impact of four laws on the activity of radical eco-groups produced mixed results. The tree-spiking clause of the Anti-Drug Abuse Act (ADA) decreased environment-only attacks but increased the hazard of animal-related attacks. The Animal Enterprise Terrorism Act decreased future animal-related attacks. However, neither the Anti-Terrorism and Effective Death Penalty Act nor the Animal Enterprise Terrorism Act had a significant effect on any of the outcomes. Sharvit et al. (2013) used series hazard models to assess the effects of efforts by the Israeli government on different measures of Palestinian terrorism by specific groups and found that the response to Israeli tactics varied across groups. Finally, Argomaniz and Vidal-Diez (2015) used the series hazard model to test the effects of six major efforts by the Spanish government to reduce the risk of terrorism by the Basque group ETA and found evidence that some of these efforts increased the risk of new terrorist attacks by ETA rather than deterring them.

Group-Based Trajectory Analysis

Group-based trajectory analysis was originally developed by criminologists to examine individual patterns of criminal offending beginning early in childhood and extending through adolescence and on into adulthood (Nagin & Land, 1993; Nagin & Tremblay, 1999). Group-based trajectory analysis is especially useful for exploring a long-standing issue in criminology: whether crime rates decline as individual offenders age or whether the appearance of declining crime rates with age is instead produced by a mixture of nonoffenders and offenders with varying lengths of criminal careers. LaFree, Yang and Crenshaw (2009) used GBTA to study the attack patterns of fifty-three foreign terrorist groups that were identified by the US State Department as posing a special threat to the United States. My colleagues and I produced two sets of analyses that differed in terms of whether the attacks targeted US citizens or non-US citizens and found that each study produced four distinct trajectories. Three of these trajectories distinguished three periods of rapid growth in terrorist attacks: the 1970s, the 1980s and the early twenty-first century. The fourth category included terrorist groups that attacked very infrequently during the four decades included in the analysis. Our analysis also revealed that despite being labeled as a threat to US nationals by the US government, these groups targeted the US homeland in only 3 percent of their attacks. In short, a group of foreign terrorist organizations that were avowedly anti-American in fact rarely attacked US targets!

In 2012, Miller expanded the application of GBTA by using it to examine attack patterns of terrorist groups at the beginning and at the end of their organizational careers. She studied the attacks of 557 terrorist groups in the GTD that were active for at least 365 days between 1970 and 2008. She used GBTA to build a more complete understanding of how the origins of terrorist organizations are related to their decline and demise. She found that terrorist groups that perpetrate attacks at a rapid pace immediately after their onset are two to three times more likely to attack frequently throughout their careers, and compared to other groups, decline at a slower rate.

Criminologists have also applied GBTA to spatial units in order to examine country-level trends in terrorism. LaFree, Morris and Dugan (2010) examined worldwide terrorist attack patterns for 206 countries from 1970 through 2006 and found that countries could be classified into five distinct trajectory categories. Among them was a category composed of only five countries, but accounting for nearly 40 percent of all attacks. The authors point out that, as with more common crime, terrorist attacks are highly concentrated both in time and space.

Morris and Slocum (2012) updated the LaFree, Morris and Dugan (2010) study in a methodological paper that compared country-level patterns of domestic and transnational terrorism using two types of group-based analyses, latent class growth analysis (LCGA) and an alternative GBTA modeling approach based on general mixture modeling (GMM). They conclude that for the purpose of identifying hot spots of terrorist activity, LCGA results provide more useful results than GMM.

Self-exciting Point Process Methods

Self-exciting point process methods were originally developed by scholars in other disciplines (Hawkes, 1971; Ozaki, 1979), but were gradually adopted by criminologists (Mohler et al., 2011; Mohler, 2014). Self-exciting point process models are generally used to describe the intensity of some outcome (in this case terrorist attacks) based on the timing of previously occurring outcomes. The idea is that the timing of previous events may "excite" the occurrence of future events. White, Porter and Mazerolle (2013) apply SEP process models to terrorist attacks within Indonesia, the Philippines and Thailand from 2000 to 2010 to measure and compare the fluctuation of terrorist activity over time. The researchers identify three parameters describing trends in terrorist attacks: risk, resilience and volatility. They measure risk by estimating increases in the expected number of daily attacks, resilience as the length of time after an initial attack that it takes the risk of a new attack to return to its pre-event level, and volatility as the total increase in risk caused by each new terrorist attack. Their findings show that the patterns of risk, resilience and volatility differ across countries. For the three countries across the years examined, the Philippines was the riskiest and had the least resilience. Indonesia was the least risky, the least volatile and had the most resilience. Thailand was the most volatile of the three countries.

Porter and White (2012) present a variation of the SEP process model that jointly estimates the probability of an attack and the number of attacks on a given day in Indonesia as a function of the timing of previous attacks. The authors claim that this variant of the SEP process model improves predictability by rapidly adapting to changes in attack patterns and that the predictive capabilities of the SEP model can help governments more strategically allocate scarce security resources.

Analysis of Spatial and Temporal Clustering

Another set of methodological contributions that were developed in other disciplines but applied to terrorism by criminologists also identifies hot spots in terrorist activity, but in this case, by estimating the spatial and temporal clustering of events. To examine how terrorist attacks cluster spatially and temporally over time, researchers have relied on the Knox test (Knox, 1964), which uses a 2×2 contingency table to assess pairs of events according to how close they are in space and time. In the mid-1960s, researchers started using the Knox test to explore space-time clustering of different forms of cancer. Decades later, Braithwaite and Johnson (2012) used similar methods to investigate the space-time clustering of improvised explosive device (IED) attacks in Iraq using data on 3,775 IED discoveries and explosions between January and June 2005. The researchers used Knox analysis to study the connections between IED events and a wide variety of counterinsurgency activities aimed at stopping these events. They found that IED events were indeed highly clustered in space and time. After an initial IED explosion, more are likely to occur soon (two weeks or less) and nearby (within 1.5 kilometers).

In the earlier discussion of criminology theories applied to terrorism, I introduced an article by Behlendorf, LaFree and Legault (2012) that identified localized bursts of terrorist attacks (which the authors call "microcycles") for ETA attacks between 1970 and 2007 and FMLN attacks between 1980 and 1992. Behlendorf and colleagues use the Knox analysis to identify these microcycles. Because the Knox test evaluates distances in space and time between every event and every subsequent event, the authors ultimately examined the distances between 1.5 million pairs of attacks drawn from 1,762 cases for ETA and the distances between almost 3.5 million pairs of attacks drawn from 2,636 cases for the FMLN. The researchers found significant evidence for space and time interaction for five miles and two weeks from the original event. They then modeled the predictors of these "microcycles" and concluded that bombings were the predominant attack mode and that compared to nonfatal attacks, fatal attacks were less likely to be part of microcycles.

Another type of spatial analysis brought to the study of terrorism by criminologists is the use of Local Indicators of Spatial Association (LISA) statistics. They were originally developed by Luc Anselin (1995) to locate hot spots. Cohen and Tita (1999) extended the cross-sectional application of LISA statistics to identify patterns of diffusion for youth-gang homicides over time within one city. Their model distinguishes between contagious diffusion, which is diffusion across contiguous units, and hierarchical diffusion that spreads more broadly with common influences.

LaFree et al. (2012) apply temporal LISA statistics to terrorist attacks by the Basque terrorist group, ETA. The group was chosen because its campaign between 1970 and 2007 was nearly continuous, allowing for the shifts in spatial patterns to be meaningful. Further, in 1978, the group announced a change in tactics from seeking an outright military victory in the Basque region to undertaking a broader war of attrition throughout Spain. The authors interpret this tactical shift as moving from "control" attacks that take place mostly in the Basque region to "attrition" attacks that are perpetrated throughout Spain and are calculated to wear down the Spanish government. The authors define control attacks as those that spread through direct contact between spatial units in the terrorist organization's base of operations (i.e., contiguous provinces). They define attrition attacks as those that spread to more distant locations outside of the terrorist organization's operational base (i.e., to more distant, noncontiguous provinces). The authors find that following the public announcement of a change in tactics by the leadership of ETA in 1978, attacks in Spain indeed shifted from control to attrition forms of diffusion.

Perry (2020) points out that most of the prior literature examining the geospatial distribution of terrorist attacks has focused on macro-level analyses such as countries and regions while few studies have examined the micro-level distribution of attacks. He argues that this contrasts with studies of ordinary crime, where there is a large body of research on micro-level crime hot spots. To bring the advantages of micro-level spatial analysis to the study of terrorism, Perry relies on a database of terror attacks in the city of Jerusalem between 2000 and 2017. The database includes the exact geographic location of attacks involving explosives, shootings, stabbings, attacks with a deadly weapon, and attacks using vehicles. Perry's analysis shows that there is a high frequency of terror attacks concentrated in specific hot spots in Jerusalem and these hot spots are relatively stable over time. He points out that the results suggest the need for specialized counterterrorism responses equivalent to the hot spots policing strategies that often inform ordinary police work.

Hasisi et al. (2020b) analyzed vehicular terrorist attacks (where perpetrators deliberately ram vehicles into crowds, buildings or other vehicles) in relatively small neighborhoods within Jerusalem and the West Bank. Additionally, the researchers analyze the concentration of the travel routes of attackers and compare the relative concentrations of the travel routes with the attack sites. The authors find that terrorist perpetrators, like ordinary offenders, favor targets close to where they live; the number of attacks decays as the distance between the residence of the attacker and the attack increases.

Risk terrain modeling (RTM) is another recent method for analyzing spatial and temporal clustering of events. Marchment, Gill and Morrison (2020) use RTM to identify the risk factors for bombings and bomb hoaxes committed by violent dissident Republicans in Belfast, Northern Ireland. Based on their analysis, they conclude that high-risk areas for bombings were associated with previous protests and riots, spatial characteristics of the targets, punishment attacks (i.e., attacks on dissident members of the perpetrator's own community) and areas dense with pubs and bars. By comparison, bomb hoaxes were associated with punishment attacks, police stations and areas of the city that were dense with shops. Based on the observed differences between bombings and bomb hoaxes, the researchers conclude that perpetrators choose targets that are relevant to their ideology or that have a high chance of success. More generally, their results suggest that offenders assess risk and select targets rationally based on these assessments.

Network Analysis

Semmelbeck and Besaw (2020) examine terrorist networks and connections between terrorism and ordinary crime. The authors use random forest methods to predict which terrorist groups will also engage in organized crime. Briefly, random forest methods depend on machine learning techniques that are used to solve regression and classification problems. The random forest algorithm makes predictions by taking the average or mean of the output from various outputs or "trees." Increasing the number of outputs increases the precision of the prediction. Using random forest methods, Semmelbeck and Besaw show that it is the characteristics of terrorist organizations themselves rather than environmental factors that predict their involvement in organized crime. Even though the authors state that their analyses are not designed to identify causal relations, the findings are noteworthy as such organizational characteristics may easily serve as useful warnings about future behavior. Their analyses highlights how models that incorporate linear associations may miss out on the nonlinear pathways in which terrorist groups end up engaging in organized crime.

McMillan, Felmlee and Braines (2020) investigate how the structure of terrorist networks develops over time, in different phases of their formation and activities. The authors argue that these changes are guided by balancing the needs for efficiency and security in the period before attacks. The authors use information about individual terrorists and their mutual social relationships connected to eleven prominent Islamist attacks (e.g., the 2002 Bali bombings) since the 1980s. Based on network analysis, the researchers find that in the period before a violent attack, networks become increasingly well-connected and organized around key actors. These kinds of analyses may help counter-terrorism efforts by suggesting which actors in networks are the most influential targets.

Agent-Based Modeling

Two decades ago, Bankes (2002: 7199) declared that ABM represented "a revolutionary development for social science." Agent-based modeling has been gradually gaining traction in criminology, and applications to terrorism are beginning to appear. A recent example is Weisburd et al. (2022) who use agent-based models to compare the impacts of three different types of interventions targeting recruitment to terrorism – community workers at community centers; community-oriented policing; and an employment program for high-risk agents. The first two programs are social interventions that focus on deradicalization and changing the dispositions of agents in the model, whereas the employment program focuses on "deflection" and represents a situational-/opportunity-reducing approach to prevention. The results show significant impacts of the community worker and community policing interventions on radicalization but no significant impact on recruitment. In contrast, the employment intervention had a strong and significant impact on recruitment, but little impact on radicalization. The ABM analysis underscores the importance of social interventions that focus on risk and protective factors for reducing radicalization in society. The findings also suggest that policy makers should focus less on counter and deradicalization approaches and more on deflection and opportunity reduction.

Meta-analysis

A final method used frequently in criminology that has been applied to the study of terrorism is meta-analysis. A meta-analysis is a statistical analysis that combines the results of multiple scientific studies that address the same question, with each individual study reporting measurements that are expected to have some degree of error (Lipsey & Wilson, 2001). The aim is to use statistical calculations to derive a more accurate pooled estimate of the underlying relationship between some intervention and some outcome. Based on searches in English, German and Dutch, Wolfowicz and colleagues (2020) identified sixty studies containing over seventy individual models and provide a meta-analysis of risk and protective factors for three radicalization outcomes: radical attitudes, intentions and behaviors. They used random effects meta-analysis to produce pooled estimates to quantify the effects of all risk and protective factors for which they were able to identify rigorous empirical data. They next created a rank order of effect sizes to identify the relative importance of each factor. Across all three outcomes, the researchers found that the most important protective and risk factors are those associated with social control and self-control theories, specifically factors pertaining to peers, school, parenting, social integration, and attitudes towards norms and values such as legitimacy.

Methods Contributions of Criminology: Conclusions

The research methods described in this section demonstrate that criminologists have indeed contributed to the growing methodological sophistication of terrorism research. The increased application of cutting-edge methods commonly used in criminology, including many of those reviewed here, are improving the rigor of scholarship on terrorism. Moreover, the application of criminological methods offers fresh perspectives that will help us better understand terrorism and its effects. I will argue in the next section that these developments not only improve research on terrorism but also increasingly provide insights that may be usefully applied to more common areas of mainstream criminology. I next briefly consider some of the policy advantages of criminal justice responses to terrorism.

Advantages of Criminal Justice Processing

While I have focused so far in this section on how terrorism research has been enriched by incorporating theoretical perspectives and novel methodologies from criminology, there are also important advantages of applying criminal justice perspectives to countering terrorism. From a practical standpoint, it is hard to imagine any effective defense against terrorism that does not include traditional policing. At present, there are more than 800,000 full-time sworn police officers in the United States (National Law Enforcement Memorial Fund, 2021). By contrast, there are a few thousand FBI special agents working on terrorism cases (Bjelopera, 2013). As criminologist George Kelling has observed, once terrorists are in the country, "police, not the FBI or the CIA, have the best tools for detecting and prosecuting these crimes" (in Howard, 2004). This conclusion is strongly supported by Dahl (2011), whose study of why terrorist plots fail shows that the most common method for foiling domestic plots is human intelligence, and the most common form this intelligence takes is police contacts with the community (see also, Hamm, 2007).

The involvement of police and the criminal justice system in counterterrorism also has important political advantages. Policy makers generally have two major options for responding to terrorism: criminal justice and military approaches. These two approaches were starkly contrasted by US reactions to the first and second attacks on the World Trade Center (WTC) in New York City. On February 16, 1993, a truck bomb in the basement parking garage of the WTC killed six, injured hundreds and destroyed a half a billion dollars' worth of property. The US response to this attack relied on traditional criminal justice system processing. After trials and convictions, six Arab men were sent to US prisons. On September 11, 2001, a second attack on the WTC brought down the Twin Towers and, along with two other coordinated attacks, caused nearly 3,000 deaths. But unlike the mostly criminal justice response to the 1993 attack, the war on terror that began after 9/11 was followed immediately by the military invasion of Iraq and Afghanistan, the deaths of thousands, an estimated two trillion dollars in spending from the United States alone and an unfolding process that has substantially altered not only US but world history. One immediate consequence of this broad targeting was that Muslim populations both in the United States (Abdo, 2006: BO3) and elsewhere (Weber, 2006) developed increasingly negative attitudes toward the US government, which in turn made them more susceptible to extremist views advanced by radical Islamist groups.

Criminal justice responses to terrorism have clear limits. For example, it is difficult to imagine an effective reaction to the 2016 attacks of the Islamic State based only on a criminal justice response. However, a criminal justice response to terrorism also has several clear advantages. First, compared to a military approach, a criminal justice approach is more limited in scope. The targets of criminal justice investigations are individual wrong doers – not entire countries or categories of people. Second, not only is a criminal justice approach more limited in scope than a military approach, but compared to rules for military engagements, the rule of law is more specific in terms of defining the nature of the wrongs committed. Just how broad the military approach can be is illustrated by a speech made by President Bush (2001) a few days after the 9/11 attack in which he pledged that the war on terror "will not end until every terrorist group of global reach has been found, stopped and defeated." By contrast, criminal justice expectations are far narrower. No one expects crime to be totally eliminated, only managed. And finally, compared to a military approach, a criminal justice approach has more built in limitations and safeguards. While criminal justice systems are far from perfect, they offer more opportunities than military systems for balancing law enforcement against preserving civil liberties.

Although it is clear that pulling police into counterterrorism functions raises challenges, it also brings benefits. In fact, many successful investigations of terrorist groups resemble successful police operations. Stopping terrorists requires detailed, accurate, timely community-level intelligence. It requires communities that trust the police and are willing to share information with them. In short, the community-oriented approach favored by successful police departments is the same kind of approach most likely to uncover terrorist operations. Such investigations are long term, culturally sensitive and micro-level. This approach strongly contrasts with the typically short-term, macro-level orientation of conventional military operations. As Dahl (2011: 635) notes: "the most important step toward preventing future attacks is to focus on local and domestic intelligence and to figure out how to gather the necessary intelligence while still maintaining the proper balance between civil liberties and security."

Contributions of Criminology to the Study of Terrorism

As criminologists have turned their attention to the study of terrorism over the pasts several decades, we have seen growing evidence of criminological effects on terrorism research. We began this section by looking at how researchers have begun to rely on criminology theories for help in understanding terrorism. While the overall impact of criminology theory on terrorism research is still modest, major criminological perspectives such as situational and rational choice perspectives are increasingly being used to understand terrorism.

Moreover, other mainstream criminology theories, such as anomie, social control and differential association are also making inroads. An ongoing challenge in applying mainstream criminology theories to terrorism is the fact that valid individual-level data on terrorist perpetrators has not been widely available. However, this situation is changing with the growing availability of open source data on terrorist perpetrators.

Terrorism research has also benefitted from the application of research methods commonly used in criminology. Not only are theoretical perspectives and research methods from criminology being adopted by researchers interested in terrorism, but the speed of the adaptations appears to be increasing over time.

In addition, criminology has had important effects on reactions to terrorism by providing a criminal justice alternative to military interventions. While this model has definite limits, it also has crucial advantages over military responses. Perhaps most importantly, criminology tells us that crime is never eliminated, only managed. As sociological pioneer Emile Durkheim (Simpson, 1933) pointed out more than a century ago, no known society has ever existed without crime. Similarly, the goal of eliminating all terrorist attacks may not only be impossible, it may represent a situation where the cure is worse than the potential disease. Most terrorism does not present an existential threat. Terrorist attacks are rare, and mass casualty attacks are rarer still. The vast majority of individuals that claim support for terrorist goals will never engage in illegal criminal behavior for a terrorist cause. Responses to terrorism encourage immediate and far-reaching responses that are not easily rolled back. The traditional criminal justice system offers an alternative to military interventions that may provide enhanced security without seriously threatening civil liberties.

In the next two sections, I turn to explicit comparisons of terrorism and more common types of crime. In Section 3, I examine data from the United States, and in Section 4 I look at worldwide data.

3 Terrorist Attacks, Terrorist Perpetrators and Criminal Offenders in the United States

In this section, I compare terrorist attacks and perpetrators to more common types of criminal offenders in the United States. I use UCR data on homicides as a measure of ordinary crime and the Survey of Prison Inmates (SPI) as a measure of the demographic characteristics of offenders convicted of common crimes. I use the GTD to look at terrorist attacks in the United States and I rely on the PIRUS data, introduced in Section 2, to provide data on terrorist perpetrators in the United States. After comparing the characteristics of terrorist perpetrators to homicide offenders, I consider the most important variables for predicting county-level terrorist attacks and homicide rates.

The Frequency of Terrorist Attacks and Homicides in the United States

In Figure 1 I show annual trends in the total frequency of terrorist attacks and homicides for the United States, 1972–2019. Because homicide is far more common than terrorist attacks, I use two separate axes to show the results, with terrorist attacks on the left and homicides on the right. Moreover, because 1970 and 1971 are major outliers in terms of US terrorist attacks recorded by the GTD, I start the series in 1972 and discuss the 1970 and 1971 results separately.

Perhaps the first thing to notice about Figure 1 is the major difference in metrics for terrorist attacks and homicides in the United States. While terrorist attacks are generally measured in the tens, homicides are measured in the thousands. For the series as a whole, there were an average of forty-nine terrorist attacks each year compared to an average of nearly 18,000 homicides each year. At the series low point in 2006, there were only six terrorist attacks. However, despite the sizeable difference in metrics, the two series are positively (although weakly) correlated ($r = 0.35$; $p < 0.05$).

By far the largest number of total attacks recorded in the United States for a single year ($N = 468$) happened in 1970, and the second highest ($N = 247$)

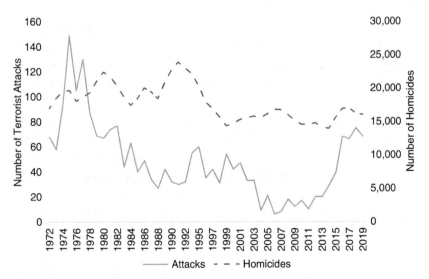

Figure 1 US terrorist attacks and homicides, 1972–2019

Sources: Terrorist attacks from the GTD; homicides from UCR data.

happened in 1971. By contrast, the highest number of homicides in the series took place in 1991 (N = 23,954) while 2014 was the year with the fewest homicides (N = 13,966). Following the large drop in attacks after 1970, total attacks hit a second peak in the mid-1970s with about 120 attacks per year. Total attacks continued to decline until reaching a series low point in 2006 (N = 6). Since 2006, attack totals have again increased, reaching a new high in 2018 (N = 75); the highest reported since 1982.

The total terrorist attacks reported in Figure 1 include only attacks on US soil. The GTD also allows us to look at how often US individuals, businesses and government installations were targeted in other countries. According to the GTD, from 1970 to 2019, there were a total of 2,638 terrorist attacks against US targets outside of the United States. Taken together, these attacks killed a total of 2,764 individuals (including 1,043 Americans) – on average about fifty fatalities per year. In order of importance, the five countries with the largest number of attacks against US targets outside of the United States were Lebanon, the United Kingdom, Italy, Iraq and Saudi Arabia. Again, the number of Americans killed by terrorists outside the United States is a tiny fraction of all homicide victims in the United States.

I next compare the top ten US cities in terms of total terrorist attacks, fatalities and homicides. According to Table 2, New York City tops the list for all three categories – the only city that shows up on all three lists. One of the most striking aspects of Table 2 are differences in the relative degree of concentration across the three categories. In particular, New York City is the location for 73 percent of all terrorism-related fatalities for the fifty years spanned by the data and of course the main explanation for this incredible concentration is the coordinated attack of 9/11. Contrasting 9/11 as a crime versus a terrorist attack highlights one of the most important differences between terrorism and ordinary crime: terrorist attacks are at once relatively rare but at the same time can result in far more casualties than result from ordinary crime.

The 9/11 attacks on the Twin Towers of the WTC by al Qaeda took 2,763 lives – nearly three-quarters of all terrorism-related fatalities in the United States from 1970 to 2019. Initially, the FBI treated the deaths that resulted from the 9/11 attacks as homicides (FBI, 2001a). But in a subsequent special report (FBI, 2001b: 302), the FBI decided to exclude the 9/11 deaths from annual homicide estimates, noting that "they are different from the day-to-day crimes committed in this country" and that "combining these statistics with our regular crime report would create many difficulties in defining and analyzing crime as we know it." The impact of this decision on annual homicide rates is substantial. The UCR recorded a total of 649 homicides in New York City in 2001. Including deaths from the attacks on the Twin Towers in New York City

Table 2 Top ten US cities for terrorist attacks and fatalities and homicides, 1970–2019

Rank	Most attacks	Percentage of total	Most attack deaths	Percentage of total	Most homicides	Percentage of total
1	New York City	16	New York City	73	New York City	6
2	San Juan, PR	4	Arlington, VA	5	Chicago	4
3	Los Angeles	4	Oklahoma City	4	Los Angeles	3
4	San Francisco	3	Las Vegas	2	Detroit	3
5	Washington, DC	3	Orlando	1	Philadelphia	2
6	Miami	3	Shanksville, PA	1	Houston	2
7	Chicago	2	El Paso	1	Baltimore	1
8	Seattle	1	San Francisco	1	Dallas	1
9	Berkeley	1	Pittsburgh	0	Washington, DC	1
10	Denver	1	San Juan, PR	0	New Orleans	1

Sources: Terrorist attacks from the GTD; homicides from UCR data.

(2,763) would more than quadruple this number. Excluding deaths from the 9/11 attacks even has a substantial impact on homicides for the whole country in 2001 – raising the total by nearly 20 percent from 15,980 to 18,976 (FBI, 2001a: 19). Note that the other two parts of the coordinated 9/11 attack are also among the top ten, which includes the 189 victims of the attack on the Pentagon in Arlington, Virginia, and the forty-four victims of the plane that crashed in a field in Shanksville, Pennsylvania. Taken together, the top ten cities in Table 2 account for 88 percent of all US terrorism-related deaths for the time period examined.

Total terrorist attacks are far less concentrated than fatalities but far more concentrated than total homicides. Thus, while 16 percent of all attacks took place in New York City, it only accounts for 6 percent of all homicides. The top ten cities for terrorist attacks account for 38 percent of all attacks, while the top ten cities for homicides account for 24 percent of the total.

According to Table 2, four cities are among the top ten in terms of both terrorist attacks and homicides: New York City, Chicago, Los Angeles and Washington, DC. Top ten cities in terms of terrorist attacks and homicides are in large part a function of population size: New York City, Los Angeles and Chicago are the three largest cities in the United States. The fourth overlap city, Washington, DC, is both a symbolic target for terrorist perpetrators and also has long had high homicide rates. A major difference between total terrorist attacks and fatalities and homicides is in the size of the top cities represented. While all ten of the top ten cities in terms of homicides are relatively large metro areas, top ten cities for terrorist attacks include much smaller cities. This again reflects the fact that terrorist fatalities are strongly concentrated. Thus, Arlington and Shanksville are on the list because of the 9/11 attacks; Oklahoma City makes the top ten because of the deadly attack in 1995 on the Alfred P. Murrah Federal Building by Timothy McVeigh; Orlando, Florida is on the top ten list because of the June 2016 mass shooting by Omar Mateen at a gay nightclub; and Las Vegas is on the list because of the October 2017 mass shooting by Stephen Paddock during a concert at the Mandalay Bay Hotel that killed fifty-nine and injured 850 more.[2]

---

[2] The FBI Behavioral Analysis Unit ultimately determined that this was not a terrorist attack because "there was no single or clear motivating factor" and that Paddock "was not seeking to further any religious, social, or political agenda." The GTD team agreed with the FBI assessment that the act did not clearly show a desire to further a political, economic, religious or social goal, but nonetheless include the attack in the database because it meets other required criteria. However, the GTD also reports that a credible witness claimed that in the weeks before the attack, she overheard Paddock espousing anger over the 1990s standoffs in Waco, Texas and Ruby Ridge, Idaho. Moreover, the GTD points out that a second witness reported that Paddock expressed concern over the US government "confiscating guns" and that "somebody has to wake up the American public and get them to arm themselves." Following past GTD practice,

Comparing Terrorist Perpetrators and Prison Inmates

In order to compare terrorist perpetrators and more ordinary types of offenders in the United States, I turn next to data on terrorist perpetrators from PIRUS data and on more ordinary types of criminal offenders from the SPI. The database PIRUS is an individual-level open source database, drawn from court documents, online news articles, newspaper archives, open source nongovernment reports (e.g., the Southern Poverty Law Center), unclassified government reports (e.g., annual FBI terrorist reports) and existing terrorism-related data sets (e.g., GTD), and contains background, demographic, group affiliation and contextual information for around 2,000 individuals who radicalized in the United States from 1948 to 2018 (for a codebook see: www.start.umd.edu/ sites/default/files/files/research/PIRUSCodebook.pdf). The individuals in the database were included for committing ideologically motivated illegal violent or nonviolent acts, joining a designated terrorist organization, or associating with organizations whose leaders have been indicted for ideologically motivated violent offenses. The database may be seen as a sample of US domestic terrorism cases in that most or all of the individuals' radicalization occurred while they were residing in the United States. To be a part of PIRUS data, each individual must meet the following inclusion criteria: (1) radicalized while living in the United States; (2) espoused or currently espouses ideological motives; and (3) shown evidence that his or her behavior was linked to the ideological motives he or she espoused.

The SPI is conducted by the Bureau of Justice Statistics and is a national survey of prisoners age eighteen or older who are incarcerated in state or federal correctional facilities within the United States. In the next sections, I compare major demographic characteristic of violent and nonviolent political extremists in the PIRUS data to prison inmates convicted of violent and nonviolent crimes in the SPI data.

Perpetrator Age

The common criminological observation that violent crime is associated with youth (Farrington, 2003; Sweeten, Piquero & Steinberg, 2013) is also commonly made in the research literature on terrorist perpetrators. For example, Pape (2005) found that the average age of offenders in his study of suicide terrorists ranged from a low of twenty-one years for the Lebanese Hezbollah to thirty years for Chechen political extremists. In Table 3, I compare the age of

---

the case is included in the database but with the caveat that ambiguities in classifying this case as a terrorist act remain.

Table 3 Age of political extremists and prison inmates

	PIRUS			SPI		
	All extremists (N = 1,724) Mean (SD)	Violent (N = 1,005) Mean (SD)	Nonviolent (N = 719) Mean (SD)	All inmates (N = 24,462) Mean (SD)	Violent (N = 10,874) Mean (SD)	Nonviolent (13,254) Mean (SD)
Age of involvement (years)	34.65 (13.62)	33.12 (13.37)	36.79 (13.68)	20.65 (9.96)	19.97 (9.67)	21.10 (10.10)

Sources: Extremist data from PIRUS (2060–2018); imprisonment data from SPI (2016).

violent, nonviolent and total political extremists in the PIRUS data. From the SPI, I compare all inmates and inmates convicted of either violent or nonviolent offenses.

What is most striking about Table 3 is that both violent and nonviolent political extremists are considerably older than both violent and nonviolent prison inmates. For both groups as a whole, this difference amounts to about ten years.[3] Similar findings have been reported in several other recent studies. For example, in an analysis of 600 American Islamist extremists, Klausen, Morrill and Libretti (2016) found that the median age for commission of violence was older and occurred across a broader age range than was the case for offenders who had committed more typical violent crimes. Similarly, in a comparison of political extremists and gang members in the United States, Pyrooz et al. (2017) found that the average age of adolescent gang members in the United States from the National Longitudinal Survey of Youth was nineteen years of age while the average age of US political extremists (from the PIRUS data) was thirty-four years old.

Other Demographic Comparisons

In Table 4, I compare a set of common demographic characteristics for violent and nonviolent political extremists from the PIRUS to convicted offenders from the 2016 SPI.

Gender. The overrepresentation of men in both crime (Gendreau, Little & Goggin, 1996; DeLisi et al., 2013) and terrorist attacks (Berrebi, 2007; LaFree et al., 2018) is well established. Nevertheless, Bloom (2017) argues that the proportion of women engaging in terrorism is increasing, and a growing literature (Sjoberg & Gentry, 2011; Bloom, 2012; Ortbals & Poloni-Staudinger, 2018) has examined forms of female participation in terrorism.

Our results generally confirm prior research on the disproportionate participation of men in both crime and terrorism. According to Table 4, men are consistently more highly represented among both violent and nonviolent political extremists and prison inmates. However, there are substantial differences across the categories being compared. Men were most common in our sample of violent political extremists, where they accounted for nearly 95 percent of all cases. They were least common among nonviolent prison inmates, where they accounted for less than 70 percent of all cases. In general, men were more highly

---

[3] The actual age difference is likely even greater because the SPI is limited to inmates eighteen years or older while the PIRUS data has no age limitation.

Table 4 Demographics of political extremists and prison inmates

	PIRUS			SPI		
	All extremists (N = 1,773)%	Violent (N = 1,018)%	Nonviolent (N = 755)%	All inmates (N = 24,013)%	Violent (N = 10,673)%	Nonviolent (N = 13,015)%
Male	90.75	94.70	85.43	74.43	81.67	68.35
Black	11.28	15.52	5.56	37.45	44.20	32.07
Hispanic	2.82	3.54	1.85	21.43	19.18	23.18
Born citizen	80.16	77.70	85.82	89.53	92.35	87.31
Married	22.84	21.32	24.90	15.76	12.83	18.20
High school	36.66	38.70	33.91	23.13	23.51	22.68
College[a]	14.61	13.16	16.56	5.33	4.07	6.29
Employed[b]	33.06	33.01	33.11	59.43	61.63	57.47
Military	10.60	11.10	9.93	6.43	8.62	4.56

Sources: Extremist data from the PIRUS (2060–2018); imprisonment data from the SPI (2016).

[a]College refers to the percentage of the sample who had completed college with a degree.

[b]For prison inmates, "employed" refers to the percentage of the sample who worked any job within thirty days of their last arrest. For PIRUS extremists, this refers to the percentage of the sample who was employed at the time of exposure.

represented across categories of political violence than ordinary crime. For both political extremists and inmates, the gender gap is greater for violent than nonviolent crimes.

Race/ethnicity. According to Table 4, there are major differences between US political extremists and prison inmates in terms of race/ethnicity. Comparing all extremists to all inmates shows that Blacks are more than three times more likely and Hispanics are nearly eight times more likely to be in the prison inmate sample than in the political extremist sample.

Born US citizen. In Table 4, I next compare whether the political extremists and prison inmates were born in the United States. Although the differences were relatively small, prison inmates were somewhat more likely than political extremists to have been born in the United States. The difference is largest among political extremists and inmates connected to violent crimes, where 92 percent of inmates but only 78 percent of political extremists were born in the United States.

Marital Status. The relationship between marital status and lower crime rates has been supported in criminology research across a variety of methodological approaches (Kirk, 2012; Bersani & Doherty, 2013), however, its relationship to extremist violence is less clear. Russell and Miller's (1977) study of terrorist profiles in eighteen countries concluded that the typical perpetrator is an unmarried male, and Berrebi (2007) found evidence suggesting married individuals are less likely to participate in Palestinian extremism, however, other scholars have reached different conclusions. For example, three-quarters of the Islamist terrorist perpetrators in Sageman's (2008) study of Islamist extremists were married. In fact, Sageman concluded that those joining Islamist organizations are frequently not fully trusted unless their wives or daughters are sisters of other terrorist perpetrators. Bakker (2006) also reported high levels of marriage among Islamist perpetrators. Shapiro (2013) found that many Islamist groups encourage intermarriage among group members to build intragroup cohesion and trust. In a recent study, Altier, Leonard Boyle and Horgan (2021) found that marriage did not act as a protective factor against extremism. In fact, in many cases, the spouse was supportive of radical behavior and marriage was found to predict recidivism.

My findings in Table 4 are generally in line with the latter results, showing that political extremists were more likely than prison inmates to be married. I hasten to add that a large part of the difference in marital status for political extremists and prison inmates is likely due to the fact that the political extremists are on average substantially older than the prison inmates and therefore have had more time to get married.

Educational Status. In general, the link between educational status and violent crime has been inconsistent (cf., Glaser, 1964; Uggen, 2000). Tauchen, Witte and Griesinger (1994) and Witte and Tauchen (2000) found no significant link between educational attainment and crime after controlling for several individual characteristics. Similarly, Grogger (1998) found no relationship between education and crime after controlling for wages. In contrast, using data from the National Longitudinal Survey of Youth, Lochner and Moretti (2004) found that schooling significantly reduced the probability of incarceration and arrest. Other researchers (Witte & Tauchen, 2000; Gottfredson, 1997) found that time spent in school significantly reduced criminal activity.

Arnold and Kennedy (1988) apply similar arguments to their discussion of education as a factor discouraging participation in terrorism. But, thus far, these expectations have received little empirical support. Indeed, the findings from much prior research (Krueger & Malečková, 2003; Pape, 2005; for a review, see LaFree & Ackerman, 2009) show that those who participate in terrorist actions are, if anything, somewhat better educated than the general population. For example, Sageman (2004) found that members of Islamist terrorist organizations were generally well educated compared with their compatriots: more than 60 percent had some education beyond high school. Similarly, Russell and Miller (1977) studied eighteen non-Muslim terrorist groups (including the Japanese Red Army, Germany's Baader–Meinhof Gang and Italy's Red Brigades) and found that, overwhelmingly, group members were well educated, with approximately two-thirds having at least some university education. Berrebi's (2007) analysis of Hamas and the Palestinian Islamic Jihad found that both group-affiliated individuals and suicide bombers were far more likely than average Palestinian citizens to have obtained a secondary or postsecondary school education.

The results in Table 4 support those researchers who claim that educational attainment is generally higher for political extremists than ordinary prison inmates. For the full sample, nearly 37 percent of the political extremists have at least a high school education compared to just over 23 percent of the prison inmates. Compared to the prison inmates, the political extremists are nearly three times more likely to have a college degree.

Employment Status. The link between various measures of employment and crime is one of the most comprehensively researched areas in criminology, and many (but not all) studies conclude that the less consistent the work history, the higher the levels of criminal activity (Smith, Devine & Sheley, 1992; Uggen, 2000). Similar arguments have been applied to discussions of the causes of terrorism (Arnold & Kennedy, 1988; LaFree & Ackerman, 2009). However, thus far, empirical results have been less convincing than support for connections between unemployment and more ordinary types of crime. Research specifically examining the relationship between employment status and participation in terrorism has found that many members of organizations that use terrorism have jobs. For instance, Hewitt (2003) found that members of the Ku Klux Klan had a diverse range of positions, from blue-collar laborers to business owners. Similarly, Sageman (2004) concluded that, at the time extremists joined Islamic terrorist groups, the majority of them were students, worked as professionals (e.g., doctors, engineers) or performed semiskilled labor.

Other research (Krueger, 2007; Silke, 2008) shows that those who participate in terrorist acts are frequently not the poorest members of their societies. An early study by Russell and Miller (1977) compiled profiles of more than 350 individual terrorist cadres and leaders across eighteen different terrorist groups from the years 1966 to 1976. The authors concluded that the majority of these individuals had middle-class backgrounds. Sageman's (2004) survey of 172 members of Islamist terrorist groups found that about three-quarters came from upper- or middle-class backgrounds. Just over one-quarter (27%) came from working-class or poor backgrounds.

However, some recent research does report a positive relationship between unemployment and terrorism. In a recent US study, LaFree et al. (2018) found that a lack of stable employment was a strong risk factor for engaging in violent political extremism. My colleagues and I measured lack of stable employment by looking at those who were unemployed as well as those who alternated between periods of employment and unemployment and those who habitually changed careers in the years leading up to their involvement in extremism.

According to Table 4, prison inmates, both those convicted of violent and nonviolent crimes, are considerably more likely than political extremists in the PIRUS data to be employed. Employment data for the inmates refers to those who report working in any job within thirty days of arrest. Employment in the PIRUS data refers to the individual's employment status at the time of exposure.

Military Background. Theories of informal social control in criminology argue that military service, along with marriage and employment, is a positive turning point that can disrupt criminal trajectories (Bouffard, 2003; Bouffard & Laub, 2004). This conclusion is generally supported in the empirical literature, with studies showing that military service is positively related to a substantial number of positive outcomes, such as economic well-being, job stability and desistance from crime (Bouffard, 2003; Bouffard & Laub, 2004).

By contrast, we could not identify any comparable literature in which the reported results show that military service is associated with lower rates of participation in political violence. In fact, preliminary evidence suggests that military service may be positively associated with extremist behavior. For example, some government reports (FBI, 2008; Department of Homeland Security, Office of Intelligence and Analysis, 2009) have detailed the risk of far-right recruitment activities in the US military. Moreover, there is evidence that military training increases rather than diminishes participation in terrorism among extremist Islamists (Cooley, 2002; Hafez, 2008). Indeed, Mendelsohn (2011) argues that individuals with military training are often specifically recruited by extremist groups because of their useful skillset, whereas those without military training are deemed to be less desirable.

In support of those who argue that military experience may have a different impact on engaging in terrorism rather than ordinary crime, Table 4 shows that political extremists from the PIRUS sample are considerably more likely than prison inmates to have a military background. Interestingly, a military background is also more common for individuals who have engaged in violent crime – both for the political extremists and the prison inmates.

County-Level Frequency of Terrorism and Homicide

In the next section, I use data from the GTD and the UCR to compare county-level frequencies of terrorist attacks and homicides. Linking terrorist attacks and homicides at the county level allows me to examine how well a common set of criminological predictors of crime work when applied to political extremism. The results are shown in Table 5.

In general, Table 5 shows both similarities and differences between the determinants of terrorist attacks and homicides at the county level. Both terrorist attacks and homicides are significantly more common in counties with a high percentage of Hispanics, that are more urban, that have a high proportion of foreign born residents and that have great language diversity. Table 5 shows that both terrorist attacks and homicides are significantly less common in counties with a high percentage of unemployed residents. Although terrorist attacks are significantly more common in counties with a high percentage of young men (aged fifteen to twenty-five), the percentage of young men is not correlated with homicide counts. Terrorist attacks are also less likely in counties with greater poverty, but the association of the poverty measure and homicide is not significant. On the other hand, although counties with a high proportion of Black residents and residents on public assistance have significantly higher homicide rates, neither variable is significantly associated with terrorist attacks.

The results are interesting in that two common measures of social disorganization, foreign born percentage and language diversity, are strongly correlated

Table 5 Bivariate correlations between county-level frequency of terrorism and homicide, 1990–2010

Variable	Terrorist attacks	Homicides
% Male, aged 15–24	0.0641*	0.0308
% Black	0.0373	0.1216*
% Hispanic	0.1358*	0.1302*
Poverty[a]	−0.0444**	−0.0055
Female-headed households	0.0145	0.0270
Unemployed	−0.0880*	−0.0791*
Public assistance	0.0297	0.0484*
% Urban	0.2555*	0.2255*
% Foreign born	0.3172*	0.2864*
Language diversity[b]	0.2340*	0.2216*

Note: *p<0.01; **p<0.05.

Sources: Terrorist attacks from GTD; homicides from 2019 UN Office of Drugs and Crime (UNODC) data.

[a]Poverty measures households with accummulated incomes below the poverty level in the past twelve months.

[b]Language diversity is calculated using the Herfindahl index. This measure captures the following languages spoken at home: Spanish or Spanish Creole; French (including Patois, Cajun); French Creole; Italian; Portuguese or Portuguese Creole; German; Yiddish; other West Germanic languages; Scandinavian languages; Greek; Russian; Polish; Serbo–Croatian; other Slavic languages; Armenian; Persian; Gujarati; Hindi; Urdu; other Indic languages; other Indo-European languages; Chinese; Japanese; Korean; Mon–Khmer; Cambodian; Hmong; Thai; Laotian; Vietnamese; other Asian languages; Tagalog; other Pacific Island languages; Navajo; other Native North American languages; Hungarian; Arabic; Hebrew; African languages; other and unspecified languages.

with both terrorist attacks and homicide counts. By contrast, two measures commonly linked to macro-level studies of homicide, public assistance and Black percentage, have no significant correlation with terrorist attacks. And poverty, a measure commonly used to explain homicide, is instead associated with fewer terrorist attacks.

I should hasten to emphasize that these comparisons are all based on data aggregated to the county level. This means that I cannot speak to the potential influence of individual criminal motivations or perpetrator characteristics. It also means that I cannot unambiguously determine whether, for example, the import-ance of population heterogeneity is a result of changes in policing, changes in the quality of informal social controls, perpetrator behavior or some combination of all these factors. Moreover, given the county-level nature of the analysis, I cannot distinguish between group-level and individual-level explanations. For example, increased language diversity could be associated with the increased frequency of terrorist attacks and homicides because counties with greater language diversity are more frequently targeted by criminal perpetrators, because terrorist attacks and homicides are more often committed by those living in counties with greater language diversity, (either by those who speak less common languages or by those who do not), because counties characterized by high levels of language diversity raise unique challenges for law enforcement resulting in less effective prevention, or because a combination of these factors causes an increase in terrorist attacks and homicides.

In fact, there is evidence supporting several of these possibilities. For instance, Disha, Cavendish and King (2011) show that county-level hate crimes directed against Arabs and Muslims significantly increased after the September 11 attacks. Relatedly, Clarke and Newman (2006) argue that because terrorist operations are resource-dependent, efforts to maximize efficiency without increasing the risk of capture suggests that groups will seek to minimize the distance traveled between events, and to the extent that foreigners are perpetrating attacks, they are more likely to do so within areas that include heavy concentrations of other foreigners (see also, Townsley, Johnson & Ratcliffe, 2008). Geographic proximity might also make recruitment of new members easier and facilitate the dissemination of ideology.

Finally, much research (Greene & Herzog, 2009; Tyler, Schulhofer & Huq, 2010) has shown that policing success depends on winning the trust and support of the local community and that population heterogeneity is likely to provide a hindrance to gaining such trust (Hill, Hubal & Gowen, 2010). Population heterogeneity may be associated with communication difficulties in general and specifically with less successful interactions with the police. Communication difficulties with officials are often cited to explain why natural disasters have significantly greater impact on immigrant than on nonimmigrant communities (Khasu, Busch & Latif, 2005; Shiu-Thornton et al., 2007). Research (James, Hawkins & Rowell, 2007; Marsella et al., 2008) has also shown that compared with native-born residents, immigrants are less likely to cooperate with authorities, including police. Many immigrants to the United States come from communities abroad in which there are few incentives for cooperating with police. Menjívar and Bejarano (2004) and others (Culver, 2004; Rosenbaum et al., 2005) show that previous negative experiences with police strongly influence current attitudes.

Conclusions: Terrorist Perpetrators and Criminal Offenders in the United States

The purpose of this section was to compare the characteristics of terrorist perpetrators and more common criminal offenders in the United States and also review some of the common responses to terrorist perpetrators and more common offenders in the United States and in other countries responding to terrorism. Perhaps the most obvious difference between terrorist perpetrators and ordinary criminals is that the latter are far more common than the former. While the United States has witnessed an average of about fifty terrorist attacks each year for the past half century, the UCR reports an average of nearly 18,000 homicides a year and, as we saw in Section 1, in 2019 alone, the UCR reported more than eight million Part I crimes. Trends in the frequency of terrorist attacks and homicides are positively correlated but weakly so. Terrorist attacks in the United States were most common in the 1970s and then steadily declined until about 2012, at which point they have increased to the present, remaining substantially under the levels observed in the early 1970s. By contrast, homicide rates increased slowly until reaching a peak in 1991, at which point they have gradually declined, but have again started to increase in recent years. Total terrorist attacks and fatalities are more concentrated than homicides at the city level. New York City is unique for having the largest portion of terrorist attacks, fatalities and homicides. In general, compared to terrorist attacks and fatalities, homicides are more closely concentrated in big cities. Thus, the top three cities for homicide in terms of percentage of the total are also the three largest cities in the United States (New York City, Los Angeles and Chicago). Compared to homicides, high concentrations of terrorist attacks are more often tied to a single deadly event, such as the 9/11 attacks that included Alexandria, Virginia and Shanksville, Pennsylvania, or the Timothy McVeigh attack on the federal building in Oklahoma City.

In order to compare the characteristics of terrorist perpetrators to ordinary criminals, I examined political extremists from the PIRUS data and inmates convicted of either violent or nonviolent offenses from the SPI. Perhaps the most striking difference is that those arrested or convicted for various types of political extremism are considerably older than those serving time in prison for ordinary offenses. The political extremists in PIRUS were more than ten years older than both the violent and nonviolent inmates in the SPI.

I found both similarities and differences between political extremists and prison inmates in terms of demographic characteristics. Political extremists and prison inmates were overwhelmingly male, although male percentage was considerably higher for the extremists (91 percent) than the inmates (74 percent). I found striking differences in terms of the racial/ethnic composition of political extremists and prison inmates. African-Americans were about three and a half times and Hispanics were about two times more likely to be in prison than to be among the political extremists in PIRUS. For Blacks, the biggest difference was for nonviolent political extremists (6 percent) compared to violent prison inmates (44 percent). More than four-fifths of both political extremists and prison inmates were born US citizens, although political extremists were somewhat less likely than inmates to have been born in the United States (80 percent versus 90 percent). Both groups had relatively low rates of marriage, however, extremists were more likely to be married than inmates (23 percent versus 16 percent). Extremists had considerably higher educational attainment than inmates: 37 percent of extremists had a high school degree compared to 23 percent of inmates; 15 percent of extremists had a college degree compared to 5 percent of inmates. Compared to extremists, prison inmates were considerably more likely to be employed shortly before their arrest (59 percent versus 33 percent). Finally, political extremists were more likely than inmates to have had military experience (11 percent versus 6 percent).

Note that an important factor in interpreting these comparisons is the relative age of the two groups. Recall that in the aggregate the political extremists are considerably older than the prison inmates. Age might be at least a partial explanation for the fact that compared to inmates, extremists are more likely to be married, to have higher educational attainment and to have served in the military.

Based on county-level data, I found a number of similarities in correlations between demographic characteristics of residents and frequency of terrorism and homicide in the United States. Both terrorist attacks and homicides were significantly more common in counties with a high Hispanic percentage, a high urban percentage, a high foreign-born percentage and great language diversity. Both terrorist attacks and homicides were significantly less common in counties with high rates of unemployment. However, I also found notable differences between county-level correlations between demographic characteristics and the frequency of terrorist attacks and homicides. While male percentage, aged fifteen to nineteen was significantly associated with terrorist attacks it had no connection to county-level homicide rates. Conversely, although Black percentage was significantly associated with homicide counts, it had no relationship to the frequency of terrorist attacks. Percentage of residents on public assistance was a significant predictor of homicides but had no impact on terrorist attacks. Terrorist attacks were significantly less likely in counties with a high proportion of residents living in poverty, while poverty was not associated with homicide frequencies.

In this section I compared terrorist attacks and perpetrators to more common types of criminal offenders in the United States. A striking finding from this comparison is that terrorist attacks are at once relatively rare but at the same time can result in far more casualties than result from ordinary crime. Although both prison inmates and political extremists are disproportionately likely to be young, political extremists are considerably older than prison inmates – about ten years older in the comparison presented here. Compared to political extremists, prison inmates are more likely to be Black or Hispanic, born in the United States, and employed; and less likely to be men, married, have a high school or college education, and be past members of the military. In county-level comparisons, both homicides and terrorist attacks were higher in counties with a higher urban percentage, a higher foreign-born percentage and greater language diversity. Common economic stress measures like public assistance and female-headed households had no impact on terrorist attack counts.

4 Worldwide Terrorism and Crime

In this section, I compare worldwide terrorism and crime. I lead off with a brief history of efforts to produce data on both topics. I rely on the GTD for data on terrorist attacks and fatalities and the World Health Organization (WHO) mortality database for data on homicides.

The Development of Open Source Terrorism Databases

As noted in earlier sections, social science in general and criminology in particular was slow to start treating terrorism as a focus for research. Moreover, as I explained earlier, the scientific study of terrorism has been hampered by the fact that none of the three major sources of crime data available to criminologists – official data from police and other legal agents and surveys of crime victims and criminal offenders – are very useful for providing cross-national evidence on terrorism patterns. However, as we saw in Section 2, open source data, unclassified data drawn mostly from the print and electronic media, have provided terrorism researchers with a major new data source. The rise of open source data on terrorism was itself related to the invention of satellite technology and hand-held portable cameras. With these advances, it was possible for the first time in human history for individuals connected to electronic media to receive news stories in real time from across the world. Starting in the late 1960s, terrorist attacks happening anywhere could be recorded and distributed to any country with the technological means to receive them.

These developments were not missed by terrorist organizations. On July 22, 1968, three armed members of the Front for the Liberation of Palestine-General Command (PFLP-GC) hijacked an El Al commercial flight scheduled to fly from Rome to Tel Aviv. The hijackers diverted the El Al plane and its forty-eight occupants to Algeria, releasing some passengers but holding five Israeli passengers and seven crew members hostage. The PFLP-GC subsequently demanded the release of Palestinian guerillas being held in Israeli prisons in exchange for these hostages. The resulting negotiations were broadcast live around the world.

In many ways, this event marked the birth of worldwide terrorism event databases. In a recent review, Bowie (2017) identifies sixty such efforts and classifies forty-three (71.7 percent) of these as primarily academic or think tank products, ten (16.7 percent) as commercial databases available for a fee and seven (11.7 percent) as government products. The duration and scope of these databases varies greatly. Many of those listed by Bowie are limited to a single country (e.g., Canadian Network for Research on Terrorism, Security and Society), region (e.g., South Asian Terrorism Portal) or are commercial endeavors unavailable to academic researchers (e.g., Jane's Terrorism and Insurgency Event Database). Others focus on terrorist groups (e.g., Big, Allied and Dangerous Database) or perpetrators (e.g., Extremist Crime Database) rather than terrorist attacks. In Table 6 I provide a summary of just those databases that include worldwide data on terrorist attacks, have been available to scholars and have resulted in published research.

Several of the databases summarized (e.g., ITERATE, GTD, DSTAT) were undertaken mostly for research purposes. The Pinkerton Global

Table 6 Worldwide open source event databases on terrorist attacks

Database	Scope	Period	Number
ITERATE	International	1968–2020	15,354
RAND	International	1968–1997	8,509
PGIS	Domestic and international	1970–1997	67,179
US State Department	International	1980–2003	10,026
DSAT	Suicide attacks	1982–2019	6,597
RAND-MIPT/ RDWTI[a]	Domestic and international	1968–2009	40,129
GTD (Stage 1)	Domestic and international	1970–2011	104,658
WITS	Domestic and international	2004–2011[b]	79,795
GTD (Stage 2)	Domestic and international	1970–2019	201,183

[a]Funding for MIPT data collection ended in 2008 and, after a brief pause, RAND continued the series as the RAND Database of Worldwide Terrorism.
[b]Data reported through March 31, 2011.

Intelligence Service (PGIS) was started by a for-profit company working in security risk assessment. RAND is a nonprofit policy research institution that mostly does research for government clients. Two of the event databases in Table 6 have been collected by the US government (US State Department, Worldwide Incidents Tracking System [WITS]). The GTD has been collected by university researchers but has been funded by US government agencies (including the National Institute of Justice, the Department of Homeland Security, the State Department and the Department of Defense) and from 2012 to 2018 supplied unclassified data to the US State Department for a congressionally mandated annual report. Of the databases listed, the GTD and ITERATE have thus far generated the most academic research. In the next two sections I divide the development of terrorism event databases into two main periods of activity: the 1970s and earlier and the late 1990s and beyond.

The 1970s and Earlier

The first four databases listed in Table 6 originated during the 1970s and earlier. The ITERATE database (https://dataverse.harvard.edu/dataset.xhtml? persistentId=doi:10.7910/DVN/TH4ADJ) began coverage in 1968, includes only international attacks and has been periodically updated through 2020 (Mickolus, 2002; Mickolus et al., 2010). The RAND Corporation was an early pioneer in developing terrorism event databases and with the support of the US State Department and the Defense Advanced Research Projects Agency (DARPA), in 1972, Brian Jenkins at RAND began to develop a "Chronology of International Terrorism" dating back to 1968 (www.rand.org/nsrd/projects/ter rorism-incidents.html). Like ITERATE, the original RAND data were generally limited to international attacks.[4]

The PGIS – a corporate descendant of the famous detective agency started in the mid-1800s by Scottish immigrant to the United States Allan Pinkerton – began collecting unclassified terrorism data in the mid-1970s. The PGIS trained researchers to identify and record terrorism incidents from wire services (including Reuters and the Foreign Broadcast Information Service [FBIS]), US State Department reports, other US and foreign government reporting, and US and foreign newspapers (e.g., the *New York Times*, the British *Financial Times*). The most unique aspect of the PGIS data is that from the beginning it included domestic as well as international terrorist attacks – the only early database to do so.

---

[4] Although RAND did include cases that were arguably domestic, including cases in Israel and Palestine.

The US State Department began publishing an annual report on international terrorism in 1982 (reporting 1981 incidents), and in 1983, began calling the report "Patterns of Global Terrorism." The Patterns Report reviews international terrorist events by year, date, region and terrorist group and includes background information on terrorist organizations, US policy on terrorism and counterterrorism efforts. The Patterns Reports were generally issued a few months after each calendar year.

The Late 1990s and Beyond

As shown in Table 6, four of the terrorism event databases include domestic as well as international attacks: the RAND-MIPT/RDWTI database, the GTD (stages 1 and 2) and the WITS data. Although the Data Base on Suicide Attacks (DSAT) includes both international and domestic attacks, it is limited to suicide attacks. In April 2001, the RAND Corporation, which had been collecting terrorism data since 1968, received support from the National Memorial Institute for the Prevention of Terrorism (MIPT) – an organization funded by the US Congress to study terrorism in the wake of the Oklahoma City bombing. With considerably more resources devoted to the database, RAND staff verified much of the earlier data and in 1998 began collecting terrorism data on domestic attacks. Funding for the RAND-MIPT data collection ended in 2008. However, shortly after, RAND received additional support and continued collecting terrorism event data, now referred to as the RAND Database of Worldwide Terrorism Incidents (RDWTI).

In 2001, I was able to secure original hard copies of the PGIS terrorism data – which by then contained more than 67,000 cases from 1970 to 1997.[5] With funding from the National Institute of Justice, our team at the University of Maryland completed the verification and digitization of the original PGIS data in December 2005. This marked the beginning of the GTD (www.start.umd.edu/gtd/). In April 2006, the GTD team received funding from the Department of Homeland Security through the National Consortium for the Study of Terrorism and Responses to Terrorism (START) to extend the GTD beyond 1997. Primary data collection of the GTD for 1998–2011 was completed by two different research teams and then verified and compiled by the GTD team at START (LaFree, Dugan & Miller, 2015). Based on these procedures, in March 2009, we released an extended version of the GTD through 2007 (LaFree & Dugan, 2007). Updates were subsequently released first biennially and then annually.

DSAT was founded in 2004 at the University of Chicago and collects worldwide data on suicide attacks (Pape, Rivas & Chinchilla, 2021; https://cpost

---

[5] The PGIS lost the original 1993 data in an office move and the GTD team has never succeeded in fully restoring it.

.uchicago.edu/research/suicide_attacks/important_definitions/). DSAT defines a suicide attack as "an event in which one or more attackers deliberately kill themselves in an effort to harm or kill others." It does not include attempted suicide attacks, in which a perpetrator fails to kill him or herself, or suicide missions, in which the perpetrator may expect to be killed in an attack. Importantly, DSAT does not require that a given suicide attack qualifies as an act of terrorism but rather includes suicide attacks undertaken for any purpose. The first confirmed suicide attack according to DSAT took place in 1982 and the data have been updated through 2019. According to Table 6, DSAT includes less than 7,000 attacks.

The WITS data collected by the National Counterterrorism Center (NCTC) began in 2004 but did not provide comprehensive annual coverage until 2005. It originated because of congressional dissatisfaction with the quality of the State Department's Patterns Report. In its 2003 Patterns Report, the State Department concluded that "worldwide terrorism had dropped by 45 percent between 2001 and 2003." However, when economists Alan Krueger and David Laitin reviewed the data tables at the end of the State Department's Patterns Report for 2003, they found that the numbers in the tables did not add up and that the conclusion of the report, namely that worldwide terrorism had decreased that year, was in error and that terrorism had actually increased. When they subsequently published this information in an op-ed piece in the *Washington Post* (Krueger & Laitin, 2004b) and in an article in *Foreign Affairs* (Krueger & Laitin, 2004a), the State Department admitted that the report was wrong and retracted it. As a result of this criticism, the name of the report was changed to "Country Reports on Terrorism," the statistical data and chronology of "significant" international terrorist events was dropped, and Congress mandated that, starting in 2004, terrorism data were to be compiled by the newly created NCTC.

The WITS data were collected by NCTC from open sources manually using commercial subscription news services, the US Government's Open Source Center, local news websites reported in English and, as permitted by the linguistic capabilities of their employees, local news websites in foreign languages (Wigle, 2010: 5). Like GTD and RAND-MIPT, WITS collected both international and domestic data. From its inception, a major goal of those administering WITS was to "cast a wider net on what may be considered terrorism" (p. 5). As a result, WITS was extremely inclusive in its coverage. From 2004 to 2011, WITS reported nearly 80,000 terrorist attacks – far more than any other event database for this period. These numbers stand in stark contrast to the earlier US State Department Patterns Reports, which typically reported only several hundred international terrorist attacks per year.

The final data set included in Table 6 is the GTD Stage 2. In recent years, the explosive growth of online media availability ushered in a new wave of innovation in terms of the collection of worldwide open source terrorism data. Early efforts to collect terrorism data quickly started to rely on news aggregators like the wire service Reuters and later online aggregators like LexisNexis, Factiva and OpenSource. However, these efforts have become far more sophisticated and comprehensive over time. At present, it is fair to say that none of the major open source terrorism databases rely only on manual data collection.

Starting in 2012, the GTD team at START began to increase substantially the amount of automation used to generate the data. The team still relies on primary sources including individual news outlets such as Reuters and Agence France-Presse, as well as existing media aggregators such as LexisNexis and Factiva, but these are now continually evaluated in terms of which sources make the most valid contributions to the overall data collection effort. At present, data collection for the GTD begins with a universe of two million articles published daily worldwide in order to identify the small subset of articles that describe terrorist attacks. The GTD team uses customized search strings to isolate an initial pool of potentially relevant articles and then relies on natural language processing methods to automatically identify and remove duplicate source articles by measuring similarities between pairs of documents. In addition, the team has developed a machine learning model using feedback from trained GTD staff that classifies documents identified by the initial automated processes to determine how likely they are to be relevant to terrorism. This model is continually refined using input from the research team regarding the accuracy of the classification results. At present, approximately 15,000–30,000 articles are manually reviewed to identify attacks for each month of data collection.

One of the innovations of GTD Stage 2 is to move from data coding based on area experts (e.g., Southeast Asia, Western Europe) to rely instead on domain-specific research teams organized to collect data on specific characteristics of attacks, including location, perpetrators, targets, weapons, tactics, casualties and consequences. Each domain-specific team records information according to the ever-evolving specifications of the GTD codebook (www.start.umd.edu/gtd/downloads/Codebook.pdf). In short, the GTD team uses automated tools to process millions of documents a day but human coders to digest the information and ensure the quality of the resulting data.

The Quest for Valid International Crime Data

Modern efforts to collect cross-national comparative data on crime can be traced back to the General Statistical Congress, convened in Brussels in 1853 (Campion, 1949). Nearly a century passed before the UN in 1949 assembled a group of experts to develop a concrete plan for collecting cross-national crime statistics (Vetere & Newman, 1977). A resolution that emerged out of this meeting recommended that efforts be made to develop standard offense classifications. However, in recognition of the wide variation in legal statutes across countries, the conference report concluded that the collection and publication of crime statistics initially be limited to homicide, aggravated assault and property crime (a combination of robberies and burglaries; Ancel, 1953). In 1950, the UN followed up on these recommendations and published its first Statistical Report on the State of Crime 1937–1946. International studies of homicide based on official statistics began to appear in the mid-1960s (e.g., Quinney, 1965; Wolf, 1971).

From this modest beginning, the empirical analysis of international crime has become gradually more common, although it has remained limited for the most part to the study of homicides. This reflects the assumption that compared to other crimes, homicides are more likely to be reported to police, police are more likely to record them and criminal justice systems spend more time and resources collecting information on homicides than less serious crimes (Eisner, 2008; Aebi, 2010).

In an earlier review (LaFree, 1999), I identified thirty-four cross-national comparative homicide studies from 1965 to 1997 and found that the most common data source used by these studies was the International Criminal Police Organization (Interpol), followed by WHO, and the UN Office of Drugs and Crime (UNODC). The first Interpol report on crime was approved in 1954 and included data for 1950 and 1951. In addition to "willful murder," Interpol reports incorporated data on sexual offenses, major and minor larcenies, various types of fraud, counterfeiting and drug-related offenses. Although Interpol was the most commonly used source for data on cross-national crime at the time of my 1999 review, it had several serious flaws. First, only about three-fifths of Interpol members bothered to submit crime statistics. Second, Interpol made no systematic efforts to verify the accuracy of the data they collected from member nations. Third, Interpol did not standardize crime definitions across countries. And finally, Interpol data were only made available several years after real time.

Annual data from participating countries on total deaths and their causes began to be collected by WHO in 1951 and defined homicide as "the killing of a person by another with intent to cause death or serious injury." WHO data are unambiguous with regard to classifying attempted homicides because, by definition, only total deaths are included. However, WHO data do not distinguish between intentional and unintentional homicides and provide no information for crimes other than homicide. For some years, WHO data include deaths that resulted from police activities, but legal executions have always been excluded. Some earlier WHO reports combined homicides with war-related casualties (Vigderhous, 1978).

The UNODC began collecting comparative crime statistics in the late 1970s by sending UN member countries a questionnaire that asked them to provide data on homicide and seven other offenses for 1970–1975. Fifty nations provided completed questionnaires as a result of this original request. Subsequent UNODC surveys were distributed for five-year periods. For the countries that responded, data sources included official publications and handbooks as well as unpublished internal documents. The five-year cycle used by the UNODC meant that available data were considerably beyond real time, the data received were not systematically verified and early participation was limited mostly to Western industrial nations.

Based on the fact that WHO homicide data were limited to the total number of medically certified deaths, used the same coding rules for the cause of death among all countries and because compared to legal systems, medical systems were presumably under less pressure to under or over report crime, I concluded my 1999 review (LaFree, 1999: 133) by arguing that on balance, the WHO data "probably represent the most valid option for researchers interested in studying cross-national homicide." Indeed, Interpol stopped making its crime data publicly available in 2006 (Smit et al., 2012) and few studies before 2000 relied on UNODC data. Hence, at the turn of the twenty-first century, most researchers (Aebi, 2010; Lappi-Seppälä & Tonry, 2011; Lysova, 2020) considered WHO data to be the "gold standard" for cross-national homicide estimates. However, in recent years, the comprehensiveness of UNODC data has greatly increased (www.unodc.org/unodc/en/data-and-analysis/global-study-on-homicide.html), and as a result, a growing number of studies have begun to rely on UNODC homicide data (Rennó Santos, Testa & Weiss 2018; Kamprad & Liem, 2021). Nevertheless, there are lingering concerns about the validity of UNODC homicide data, most notably that the UNODC does not ensure that each reporting country is using the same homicide definition when it responds to the survey (Rogers & Pridemore, 2023) and continues to rely on imputed data (Kanis et al., 2017). Accordingly, I will use the WHO mortality data for the homicide analyses that follow.

Conclusions: Terrorism Data versus Crime Data

Worldwide terrorism and crime data have very different histories. Cross-national estimates of terrorist attacks get under way in the late 1960s, along with the availability of satellite technology and portable cameras. Over time, they have become more inclusive and increasingly rely on electronic rather than print media. Because open source terrorism databases are not based on official reports, they are able to include information from many countries that are missing statistics on homicide and other common crimes. Compared to these more common crimes, terrorist attacks are unique in the sense that their perpetrators are often seeking media attention and therefore want to see information on their attacks showing up in the print and electronic media. On the other hand, open source databases have all the downsides that we discussed earlier, including whether minor events get reported, whether the press pays more attention to some types of terrorism than other types and, more generally, all of the sources of misinformation associated with the media. Attempts at developing worldwide crime data began in the 1950s and slowly grew more inclusive over time. However, the most successful efforts to produce worldwide crime data have been limited to homicide and still exclude many industrializing countries.

Comparing Worldwide Frequencies of Terrorism and Homicide

In this section I compare GTD terrorism data and WHO homicide mortality data for 1970–2016. I exclude island nations with less than 100,000 inhabitants (Anguilla, Antigua and Barbuda, Aruba, Bermuda, British Virgin Islands, Cayman Islands, Dominica, Kiribati, Montserrat, San Marino, Seychelles, St. Kitts and Nevis, and Turks and Caicos Islands). Based on these procedures, I assembled a worldwide homicide database of 3,334 country-years, 1970–2016. To allow for comparative analysis, I matched terrorist attacks from the GTD for all the country-years with homicide data.

In Figure 2, I compare annual trends in worldwide homicide counts from WHO to worldwide terrorism counts from the GTD.[6] Perhaps the most striking feature of Figure 2 is just how different the metrics are for the two crimes. For the time period covered, the worldwide data includes a total of 12,553,910 homicides but only 158,132 terrorist attacks. Thus, worldwide homicide is nearly eighty times more common than terrorist attacks for the countries where comparisons are possible. Figure 2 shows that total terrorist attacks and homicides were both increasing from the beginning of the series until the early 1990s – although the increases were greater for homicides than terrorist attacks. Both series also declined together from the early 1990s until the early 2000s.

---

[6] Only seventeen countries submitted WHO data in 2016, which make trend lines for that year misleading. Thus, I exclude 2016 data from Figure 2 but include it in the other worldwide analyses.

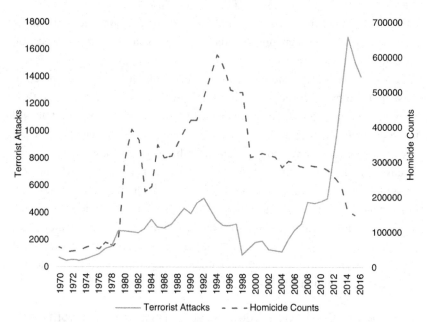

Figure 2 Worldwide terrorist attacks and homicides, 1970–2015

Sources: Terrorist attacks from GTD; homicides from the WHO mortality database.

The biggest difference in the two series occurs after the early 2000s when worldwide homicide counts continued to fall but terrorist attacks trended steeply upward. Thus, while the high point for homicides occurs in the early 1990s, the high point for terrorist attacks happens near the end of the series in 2015. Taken together, the worldwide homicide-terrorist attack series, like the US homicide-terrorist attack series, are weakly correlated ($r = 0.087$; $p < 0.10$).

In Table 7A, I compare the ten countries with the highest counts of terrorist attacks, the most deaths from terrorist attacks and the most homicides. Following prior quantitative research on terrorism, I report total event counts per country rather than rates – however, for comparison purposes, I include total population for each country in Table 7B. Countries that appear in more than one of the three lists are bolded. Only Colombia is among the top ten on all three lists. Colombia finished number five in terms of terrorist attacks, number seven in terms of terrorist fatalities and number four in terms of homicides. In general, there is far more overlap between terrorist attacks and fatalities than between either of these two and homicides. Seven of the ten countries in the top ten for terrorist attacks are also in the top ten for terrorist fatalities (Iraq, Pakistan, India, Afghanistan, Colombia, Peru and El Salvador). The Philippines, the United Kingdom and Turkey are in the top ten for total attacks but not fatalities;

Table 7A Ten countries with the most total terrorist attacks, terrorist deaths and homicides, 1970–2016

Rank	Most attacks	Count	Most deaths	Count	Most homicides	Count
1	Iraq	18,806	Iraq	59,894	Russia	6,022,417
2	Pakistan	12,783	Afghanistan	27,156	Brazil	1,374,398
3	India	9,973	Pakistan	21,633	United States	892,414
4	Afghanistan	9,702	Nigeria	18,719	Colombia	687,709
5	Colombia	8,080	India	18,411	Mexico	618,374
6	Peru	6,091	Sri Lanka	15,318	Belarus	262,249
7	Philippines	5,583	Colombia	14,561	Uzbekistan	241,103
8	El Salvador	5,320	Peru	12,754	Thailand	237,411
9	United Kingdom	5,010	El Salvador	12,053	Kazakhstan	235,045
10	Turkey	3,575	Algeria	11,044	Ukraine	178,914

Sources: Terrorist attacks from GTD; homicides from the WHO mortality database.

Table 7B Average population, 1970–2016

Country	Population (millions)	Country	Population (millions)	Country	Population (millions)	Country	Population (millions)
India	924	Mexico	87.1	Colombia	34.7	Sri Lanka	17.3
United States	261	Philippines	66.9	Algeria	26.6	Kazakhstan	15.3
Brazil	153	United Kingdom	58.6	Peru	22.7	Belarus	9.73
Russia	142	Thailand	56.1	Uzbekistan	21.3	El Salvador	5.29
Pakistan	120	Turkey	56.1	Iraq	20.2		
Nigeria	107	Ukraine	48.9	Afghanistan	18.7		

Source: UN.

Nigeria, Sri Lanka and Algeria are in the top ten for fatalities but not attacks. With the exception of Colombia, none of the top ten for homicides are also top ten for either attacks or fatalities.

Table 7B shows total population for the countries included in the figure. Despite its huge population, India is not in the top ten for homicides. Likewise, despite its relatively large population, Brazil is not in the top ten for either terrorist attacks or fatalities. By contrast, despite their relatively small populations, El Salvador is among the top ten for terrorist fatalities and Belarus is among the top ten for homicides.

Determinants of Worldwide Terrorism and Homicide

In the next section I compare the most important macro-level predictors of worldwide terrorist attacks and homicides. I start with an empirical analysis based on the comparative terrorism-homicide database considered in the last section. This analysis allows me to look at most of the common explanations of both terrorism and homicide, including youth percentage, economic development, income inequality, poverty, urban percentage, strength of democracy, fragile states, ethnic fractionalization, globalization and total population. Table 8 shows the bivariate results.

According to Table 8, seven of the ten variables examined here are significantly associated with terrorist attack counts and eight of the ten are significantly associated with homicide counts. For the seven variables that are significantly associated

Table 8 Bivariate correlations for terrorist attacks, homicides and macro variables, 1970–2016

Variable name	Frequency of terrorism	Frequency of homicide
Youth (age fifteen to twenty-four)	0.064*	0.1546*
GDP	0.033**	0.1048*
Inequality	−0.025	0.1575*
Poverty	−0.02	0.037
Urban percentage	0.004	0.0398***
Democracy	0.082*	−0.0184
Fragile states	0.242*	0.185*
Fractionalization	0.033**	0.1109*
Globalization	−0.095*	−0.0472**
Population	0.156*	0.4217*

Note: *p<0.001; **p<0.01; ***p<0.05

Sources: Terrorist attacks from GTD; homicides from WHO Mortality database.

with terrorist counts, six are also significant, and in the same direction for homicide counts. Strength of democracy is associated with higher terrorist attack counts, but not high homicide counts. These are of course only bivariate results, but it could be that the insignificant results for strength of democracy on homicide is due to the fact that transitional democracies, rather than full democracies have the highest homicide rates (LaFree & Tseloni, 2006).

In the next several sections, I consider one at a time each of the variables presented in Table 8.

Youth Percentage

The size of the youth population is a frequent measure in cross-national studies of homicide (Nivette, 2011) but is rare in cross-national studies of terrorism (Morris & LaFree, 2017). Most studies of terrorism that include age as a variable (Klausen, Morrill & Libretti, 2016; Pyrooz et al., 2017) are micro-level studies focused on terrorism perpetrators. Nonetheless, as can be seen in Table 8, we find that both terrorism and homicide are significantly more common in countries with a high proportion of individuals aged fifteen to twenty-nine.

Economic Development

Economic development, usually measured as GDP, has been a common measure in both studies of terrorism (Fahey & LaFree, 2015) and homicide (Pridemore, 2008; Messner, Raffalovich & Sutton, 2010), and for both, results have been inconsistent. Findings from several studies show that countries with high economic growth and strong welfare measures experience fewer terrorist attacks (Krieger & Meierrieks, 2012; Choi, 2015). For example, Gries, Krieger and Meierrieks (2011) find that economic success significantly reduces terrorist violence in three of the seven Western European countries included in their sample. However, based on a sample of twelve West European countries (1994–2007), Caruso and Schneider (2011) find that expected future economic growth is associated with an increase in current terrorist activity. Similarly, LaFree and Bersani (2014) find that terrorist attacks are *less* common in US counties with high levels of concentrated economic disadvantages. In another US study, Varaine (2020) finds that far-right perpetrators mobilized more frequently under periods of long-term economic deprivation, whereas far-left terrorism was more prevalent under improving economic conditions. Still other studies find either no effect (Abadie, 2006; Kurrild-Klitgaard, Justesen & Klemmensen, 2006) or a curvilinear effect (Enders, Sandler & Gaibulloev, 2011) of economic development on terrorism.

Per capita GDP is likely the single most commonly examined variable in quantitative studies of cross-national homicide (LaFree & Kick, 1986; Messner,

Raffalovich & Sutton, 2010). Several prior studies (Bennett, 1991; Ortega et al., 1992) find that homicide rates increase along with GNP or GDP. However, a meta-analysis by Nivette (2011) finds no effects for GNP. I obtained time-series data for GDP from the Penn World Table 9.1 (Feenstra, Inklaar & Timmer, 2015). According to Table 8, increases in GDP are associated with significant increases in both the frequency of terrorist attacks and homicides.

Income Inequality

Many studies over several decades support the conclusion that country-level income inequality is associated with high homicide rates (Nivette, 2011; Baumer & Wolff, 2014). Krieger and Meierrieks (2019) show that high levels of income inequality are associated with an increase in domestic terrorism, whereas redistributive efforts reduce terrorist activity. Piazza (2011) and Enders and Hoover (2012) both look at the impact of inequality (the GINI index) on terrorist attacks and fatalities and find that it is associated with high rates of attacks and fatalities.

I obtained an inequality measure (the GINI index) from the Standardized World Income Inequality Database (Solt, 2016). The results for inequality shown in Table 8 are in line with prior research on homicide but not terrorism: I find that inequality is associated with a significant increase in the former but no effect on the latter.

Poverty

Poverty is among the most widely studied, and most controversial, macro-level predictors of both homicide and terrorism. A link between area poverty and homicide is a consistent finding in most individual-level criminological research (Pratt & Cullen, 2005; Pridemore, 2008), however, the poverty–crime link is much less common in cross-national research. Moreover, most cross-national research on homicide that indicates a theoretical interest in poverty often measure it by using GDP, which we have already considered earlier. We also find little agreement about the extent to which economic measures like poverty increase terrorist attacks. The relationship between measures of poverty and terrorist attacks are significantly reduced once country-specific characteristics and measures of good governance and political freedom are taken into account, suggesting that economic stress may have indirect effects on terrorist attacks (Basuchoudhary & Shughart, 2010; Plümper & Neumayer, 2010).

For this analysis, I operationalize poverty as the percentage of the population living below the national poverty line, based on population-weighted subgroup estimates from household surveys. According to Table 8, there is no significant relationship between poverty for either terrorist attacks or homicides.

Urban Percentage

Urbanization or urban percentage has been associated with increases in terrorist attack in several prior studies (Campos & Gassebner, 2013; Danzell & Zidek, 2013). By contrast, declines in urbanization have been identified as one of the variables responsible for declining homicide rates across countries (Nivette, 2011; Baumer & Wolff, 2014). For my analysis, urban percentage measures the proportion of the population in a given country that resides in urban areas relative to the total resident population (World Bank Open Data, 2020). According to Table 8, as the proportion of the population that is urban increases, homicide counts increase, but I find no significant association between urban percentage and terrorist attacks.

Strength of Democracy

Strength of democracy is used frequently to predict country-level rates of terrorist attacks but is relatively uncommon as an independent variable in the homicide literature. An exception is LaFree and Tseloni (2006), who analyze homicide trends in forty-three nations and find that during the second half of the twentieth century, homicide rates increased for full democracies. Nevertheless, the authors also find that violent crime rates were highest for countries transitioning between autocracy and democracy. A good deal of research has investigated the extent to which regime type and level of democratization of a country correlates with terrorism (Wilson & Piazza, 2013; Gaibulloev, Piazza & Sandler, 2017). These studies operationalize country-level democracy in different ways but generally account for some or all of the following elements: electoral processes, civil and political freedoms, levels of political participation and competition. Despite the fact that the connection between democracy and terrorism has been analyzed frequently, the true effect of democracy on terrorist attacks remains uncertain. Research has suggested both positive (Wilson & Piazza, 2013; Bell, 2017) and negative relationships (Li, 2005; Masters & Hoen, 2012; Simpson, 2014) between measures of democracy and terrorism, with some studies finding no linkage between the two (Piazza, 2008a). Still other research (Abadie, 2006; Gaibulloev, Piazza & Sandler, 2017) points to a curvilinear, and more specifically to an inverted U-shaped, relationship between different measures of democracy, such as political freedom and terrorism.

My measure of democracy is the "polity score," which classifies countries on a twenty-one-point scale ranging from full autocracy to consolidated democracy (Jaggers & Gurr, 1995). Bivariate results in Table 8 confirm findings by other research (Chenoweth, 2013; Piazza, 2013), showing that as regimes transition toward more democratic systems, they experience high levels of political violence. However, the connection between strength of democracy and homicide is not significant.

Fragile States

A good deal of terrorism research has examined connections between terrorist attacks and fragile or weak states (LaFree, Digan & Fahey, 2008; Piazza, 2008b), however, I am unaware of any similar studies of cross-national homicide. In general, fragile states are defined as those that experience prolonged periods of civil conflict and war, political crises, and massive human rights violations (Esty et al., 1995: 1). Most of this research concludes that fragile states provide an ideal environment for terrorist organizations (Savun & Phillips, 2009; Bell, 2017). Nonetheless, not all research is supportive of this association (Eubank & Weinberg, 2001; Piazza, 2008b).

I examine the Fragile States Index (Messner de Latour et al., 2020), which is based on twelve conflict risk indicators that measure the stability of a state at any given moment, including group grievance, economic decline, human rights, and rule of law and external intervention. According to the bivariate results in Table 8, both terrorist attacks and homicides are significantly more common in states experiencing high fragility rates.

Religious, Ethnic and Linguistic Diversity

Religious motives have frequently been examined as a cause of terrorism (Stern, 2002; Juergensmeyer, 2003), and various measures of religion have also been used in studies of cross-national homicide (Hansmann & Quigley, 1982; Groves, McCleary & Newman, 1985). Egger and Magni-Berton (2019) use survey data collected in twenty-one European countries to investigate the link between religious beliefs and terrorism justifications among European Muslims. They find that in countries affected by homegrown terrorism, Muslims who adhere to frequent religious practice show high levels of support for terrorism. In a study of worldwide terrorist attacks, Piazza and LaFree (2019) find that compared to attacks by nonreligious groups, attacks carried out by religious groups produce more casualties. Overall, prior research agrees that there are no consistent links between specific types of religions and propensity to engage in terrorism (Kurrild-Klitgaard, Justesen & Klemmensen, 2006; Krueger & Laitin, 2008).

Due to the difficulty of distinguishing religious from secular motivations, other researchers have focused on the relationship between measures of ethnic or linguistic fractionalization and homicide (Avison & Loring, 1986; Krahn, Hartnagel & Gartrell, 1986) and terrorist attacks (Pape, 2005; Moghadam, 2006). This research reports mixed results. Whereas Kurrild-Klitgaard Justesen and Klemmensen (2006) find no significant association for measures of ethnic and linguistic fractionalization and terrorist attacks, Piazza (2011) and Foster, Braithwaite and Sobek (2013) find that countries with a more ethnically homogeneous population generate fewer terrorist attacks. According to Piazza (2012), minority socioeconomic discrimination is a particularly important predictor of terrorist activity. Basuchoudhary and Shughart (2010) show that high levels of ethnic tension are associated with high levels of terrorism. Choi and Piazza (2016) find that domestic terrorism occurs more frequently in countries that exclude certain ethnic groups from political power. Python, Brandsch and Tskhay (2017) investigate the link between ethnic tensions and terrorist attacks and find that areas with high levels of ethnic polarization experience more terrorist attacks.

Taken together, these studies point to links between identity-related measures and terrorist outcomes. However, as Krieger and Meierrieks (2012) note, many of these studies have measurement weaknesses. For example, several studies use time-invariant proxies to measure identity conflict and ethno-demographic inequality (e.g., indices for ethnic and religious fractionalization) or rely on variables indicating simple proportions (e.g., the share of the Muslim population). It is unclear to what extent these measures adequately capture tensions rooted in identity conflict, ethno-demographic diversity or group-specific grievances.

To measure fractionalization, I use data obtained from the Historical Index of Ethnic Fractionalization Dataset (Dražanová, 2019), which defines fractionalization as the likelihood that two randomly selected individuals drawn from the population belong to two different ethnic groups. According to Table 8, high ethnic fractionalization is associated with high frequencies of both terrorist attacks and homicides.

Globalization

Bove and Böhmelt (2016) and others (Blomberg & Hess, 2006; Brockhoff, Krieger & Meierrieks, 2015) assess effects of globalization on terrorist attacks through increased migration flows, international cooperation and advances in educational attainment. Several studies (Forrester et al., 2019; McAlexander, 2020) have analyzed the relationship between immigration and political violence, finding mixed results. Bove and Böhmelt (2016) find that migrant inflows generally reduce the number of terrorist attacks. However, terrorism does diffuse to other countries through migrants leaving from terrorist-prone states. Choi and Salehyan (2013) show that countries with many refugees are more likely to experience terrorist attacks. However, drawing on bilateral migration data for 170 countries from 1990 to 2015, Forrester et al. (2019) find no evidence in support of the thesis that immigrants import terrorism.

With few exceptions (Levchak, 2015; LaFree & Jiang, 2022), globalization has not been examined in cross-national studies of homicide. However,

Levchak finds partial support for some forms of globalization and LaFree and Jiang find strong support for the conclusion that as worldwide globalization increases (measured as trade openness), homicide declines. According to Table 8, high levels of globalization (measured here as trade openness) are significantly related to a low frequency of both terrorist attacks and homicides.

Population Size

Most prior studies find that compared to countries with fewer people, more populous countries experience higher levels of terrorist activity (Plümper & Neumayer, 2010; Coccia, 2018). Some scholars (Freytag et al., 2011; Ezcurra & Palacios, 2016) argue that large populations correlate with high levels of demographic stress, which in turn fosters conflict and violence. By contrast, Krieger and Meierrieks (2012) claim that terrorist attacks may simply be more likely to occur in large countries.

Population size has also been included in many cross-national studies of homicide (Messner, 1982; Shichor, 1990) and usually does not have a significant effect. For example, this is the conclusion reached in Nivette's (2011) meta-analysis of important predictors of homicide. However, most cross-national studies of homicide are based on rates rather than counts. Thus, in these studies, population size is already built into the dependent variable. By contrast, Table 8 compares total frequencies of terrorist attacks and homicides. In the analysis of frequencies, population size is significantly associated with both high frequencies of terrorist attacks and homicides.

Conclusions: Determinants of Worldwide Terrorism and Homicide

Taken together, the results in Table 8 suggest that comparisons of the determinants of worldwide terrorism and homicide might be a fertile area for future research. Of the ten variables examined, six were statistically significant and in the same direction in predicting both the frequency of terrorism and homicide: five positive and one negative. Both terrorist attacks and homicides were more common when countries had a high proportion of young persons, high GDP, had a fragile or weak state, had high ethnic fractionalization, and had large populations. Both terrorist attacks and homicides were less common when countries had high levels of globalization. Two variables were significant for predicting homicide but had no significant effect on the frequency of terrorist attacks: countries with high inequality and a high urban percentage had a high frequency of homicides. Strength of democracy had a significant positive effect on terrorist attacks but not on homicides. Only the measure of poverty had no significant effect on either terrorist attacks or homicides.

In general, the ten macro-level variables examined here have been used more frequently in the study of terrorist attacks than homicides. Given this, it is interesting that six of these variables are significantly associated with homicides. As noted in previous sections, a major difference between terrorist attacks and more ordinary types of crime is that the former have a weaker connection to economic well-being than the latter. In the bivariate comparisons, one variable that is related to homicides but not terrorist attacks is inequality. Meanwhile, poverty had no significant effect on either terrorist attacks or homicides. I offer these bivariate comparisons as a first step toward a more exhaustive multivariate comparison of terrorist attacks and homicides.

Conclusions: Worldwide Terrorism and Crime

I began this section with an exploration of worldwide trends in terrorist attacks and crime. Although attempts to develop worldwide crime statistics began nearly a century and a half ago, at this point, the most reliable cross-national crime data are on homicide, and these data are not available for all of the world's countries. Although coverage has greatly improved over time, it remains weakest for countries in Africa and Asia. By contrast, although open source data have well-known limitations, their development has allowed researchers to develop terrorist attack estimates for all countries of the world. For comparative purposes, I started with worldwide data on countries with homicide data from the WHO mortality database and then matched terrorist attack data from GTD. The results showed some similarity in trends, especially from the 1970s to the early 2000s. I also found considerable overlap between the ten countries with the highest numbers of terrorist attacks and fatalities, but relatively little overlap with homicides. Colombia was the only country in the top ten for terrorist attacks, terrorist fatalities and homicides. In contrast, seven countries were in the top ten for both terrorist attacks and fatalities.

Bivariate correlations between worldwide counts for terrorism and homicide and a set of ten macro-level variables yielded considerable overlap. Six of the variables were significantly related to both terrorist attacks and homicides. Inequality and urban percentage were positively associated with homicides but unrelated to terrorist attacks. Strength of democracy was positively related to terrorism but unrelated to homicides, and poverty was not significantly related to either terrorist attacks or homicides.

5 Discussion and Conclusions

The expansion of criminology into the study of terrorism and political extremism since the coordinated attacks of 9/11 is arguably one of the biggest changes in the field in the past quarter century. Criminology research on terrorism moved from a relatively rare subject to a common pursuit, showing up in major journals, covered in college classrooms and filling meeting rooms at professional conferences. Why did it take mainstream criminology so long to pay serious attention to a type of behavior that seems to obviously be criminal? In part, this omission likely reflects the fact that since its origins in the early 1900s, empirical criminology has strongly focused on domestic issues. By contrast, studying terrorism quite often requires cross-national data on multiple countries and legal systems. Moreover, some characteristics of terrorism make it stand out in comparison to more ordinary types of crime. As we have seen, terrorism is not strongly associated with poverty and economic inequality, and its perpetrators rarely see themselves as criminal. I argue elsewhere (LaFree, 2022) that in this sense, terrorism more closely resembles white-collar crime than crimes like homicide and robbery. Moreover, the study of terrorism, like the study of white-collar crime, has been hindered by the fact that governments have been slow to collect relevant data on it. The purpose of this Element was to explore this major turning point in criminological history by examining the contributions that criminology has made to the study of terrorism and comparing the characteristics and determinants of terrorism and more ordinary types of crime.

Terrorism shares several important characteristics with more ordinary crime, including the natural division between criminal etiology and law enforcement and an interdisciplinary emphasis. However, differences are also apparent and include the fact that terrorist perpetrators, unlike more common criminal offenders, typically do not see themselves as criminals, are often seeking media attention and typically interpret their actions as furthering broader political goals. Moreover, the study of terrorism lacks the types of official and unofficial data that are widely available in criminology and unlike most common crimes, terrorist attacks frequently have national or even international implications.

As criminologists gradually turned their attention to the study of terrorism over the past two decades, we have seen a growing impact of criminological theories and methods on terrorism research. Major criminological perspectives, especially situational and rational choice perspectives, are increasingly being used to understand terrorism. Moreover, other mainstream criminology theories, such as anomie, social control and differential association are also making inroads. Terrorism research has benefitted from the application of research methods commonly used in criminology, including series hazard modeling, GBTA, SEP process methods, analysis of spatial and temporal clustering, network analysis, ABM and meta-analysis. Criminology has also influenced terrorism policy and research by providing a criminal justice alternative to the military model for responding to terrorism. Compared to a military approach, a criminal justice approach is more limited in scope, more specific in terms of defining the nature of wrongs committed and contains more built in protections of human rights.

At the same time, criminology has been enriched by its growing connections to terrorism studies. Terrorism research has vividly illustrated the socially constructed nature of crime, has encouraged researchers to see not only the deterrence potential of punishment but also its capacity to produce backlash, has accelerated the internationalization of criminology, and has hastened the embrace of open sources as an important form of crime data. In short, integrating political crimes into criminology encourages researchers and the public to rethink their conventional ideas about crime. The socially constructed nature of crime is fairly obvious when it comes to terrorism and political extremism, but it is applicable to all forms of crime. The possibility that harsh punishment can provoke backlash as well as deterrence is apparent in the study of terrorism, but it has great relevance for the study of all crimes. The strong comparative emphasis of research on political extremism and the pioneering use of open source data have been critical for the study of political extremism but they apply equally well to more ordinary crime.

One of the challenges of integrating the study of terrorism into mainstream criminology is that terrorism resembles ordinary crime in some ways but not in others. To get a better idea of the extent to which ordinary crime and the criminal justice system treatment of crime differs from terrorism and responses to terrorism, I undertook two empirical comparisons. In the first, I compared the characteristics and determinants of terrorist perpetrators and attacks to more common forms of crime and criminal justice processing for the United States. And in the second, I undertook a similar analysis with worldwide data.

Perhaps the most obvious difference between terrorist perpetrators and ordinary criminals is that the latter are far more common than the former. While the United States has witnessed an average of about fifty terrorist attacks each year for the past half century, the UCR reported more than eight million Part I crimes in 2019 alone. Trends in the frequency of terrorist attacks and homicides in the United States are positively correlated, but weakly so. Terrorist attacks in the United States were most common in the 1970s and then steadily declined until about 2012, at which point they have increased to the present, while remaining substantially under the levels observed in the early 1970s. By contrast, homicide rates increased slowly until reaching a peak in 1991, at which point they have gradually declined, but have again started to increase in recent years. In general, compared to terrorist attacks and fatalities, homicides are far more highly concentrated in big cities. By contrast, high frequencies of terrorism are more often tied to a single deadly event, such as the 9/11 attack that included Alexandria, Virginia and Shanksville, Pennsylvania, or the Timothy McVeigh attack on the federal building in Oklahoma City.

In terms of the characteristics of political extremists and prison inmates in the United States, the most striking difference is that those arrested or convicted for various types of political extremism are on average about a decade older than those serving time in prison for ordinary offenses. Political extremists and prison inmates in the United States resemble each other in several respects. Both extremists and inmates are overwhelmingly likely to be male, are usually born US citizens and have low marriage rates. However, I also found striking differences between the two groups. African-Americans were about three and a half times and Hispanics were about two times more likely to be in prison for ordinary crimes than to be among the political extremists in PIRUS. Extremists were far more likely than prison inmates to have completed a high school or college degree. Compared to extremists, prison inmates were considerably more likely to be employed shortly before their arrest. Compared to inmates, political extremists were more likely to have had military experience.

Based on county-level data from the United States, I found that both terrorist attacks and homicides were significantly more common in counties with a high Hispanic percentage, a high urban percentage, a high foreign-born percentage and great language diversity. Both terrorist attacks and homicides were significantly less common in counties with high rates of unemployment. However, I also found notable differences between county-level correlations between demographic characteristics and the frequency of terrorist attacks and homicides. While male percentage, aged fifteen to nineteen, was significantly associated with the frequency of terrorist attacks it had no connection to county-level homicide frequencies. Conversely, although the Black percentage was significantly associated with homicide counts, it had no relationship to the frequency of terrorist attacks. The percentage of residents on public assistance was a significant correlate of homicides but was unrelated to terrorist attacks. Terrorist attacks were significantly less likely in counties with a high proportion of residents living in poverty, but poverty had no significant association with homicides.

Worldwide terrorism and crime data have very different histories and yet both have grown more inclusive over the last two decades. Open source terrorism databases got under way in the late 1960s, along with the availability of satellite technology and portable cameras. Over time, they expanded to include domestic as well as international attacks and they have increasingly relied on electronic rather than print media. At the time that this Element was being prepared, the most extensive of these terrorism databases is GTD, containing information on over 200,000 terrorist attacks from 1970 to 2019.

Attempts at developing worldwide homicide data began in the 1950s and slowly grew more inclusive. Homicide data collected by Interpol was most commonly analyzed from the mid-1960s through the 1980s, WHO homicide data became the most common homicide data source starting in the 1990s, and recent research (Rogers & Pridemore, 2023) suggests that it is still the most valid source for cross-national homicide data.

Because open source terrorism databases do not rely on officials to report data, they are able to include information from many countries that are missing statistics on homicide and other common crimes. Compared to these more common crimes, terrorist attacks are unique in the sense that their perpetrators are often seeking media attention and therefore want to see information on their attacks showing up in the print and electronic media. On the other hand, open source databases have important limitations, including whether minor events get reported and whether the press pays more attention to some types of terrorism. Until recently, available data on homicides were limited mostly to Western-style democracies. Although it is still difficult to obtain worldwide data on crimes other than homicides, there is more extensive worldwide coverage of homicide than ever before.

In order to directly compare worldwide terrorist attacks and homicides, I merged terrorism data from GTD with homicide data from the WHO mortality database. The results show that the frequency of worldwide homicides was increasing while the frequency of worldwide terrorist attacks remained flat during the 1990s, but starting in the early 2000s, frequencies for both increased. As with comparisons between the frequency of terrorist attacks and homicides in the United States, comparing worldwide totals for the two show that frequencies of terrorist attacks are a small fraction of total homicides.

Comparing worldwide terrorist attacks and homicides showed that only Colombia was among the top ten for terrorist attacks, terrorist fatalities and homicides. Unsurprisingly, there is more overlap in the top ten lists for terrorist attacks and deaths than for homicides. Thus, seven of the top ten countries for terrorist attacks are also on the top ten list for terrorist fatalities. The Phiippines, the United Kingdom and Turkey are the only countries that are on the top ten list for attacks but not fatalities, and Nigeria, Sri Lanka and Algeria are the only countries that are among the top ten for fatalities but not attacks.

In a comparison of the bivariate correlations between terrorist attacks, homicides and a common set of macro-level variables, I found considerable similarities. Of the ten variables examined, six were statistically significant in predicting both the frequency of terrorism and homicide: five positive and one negative. Both terrorist attacks and homicides were more common when countries had a high proportion of young persons, high GDP, a fragile or weak state, high fractionalization, and large populations. Both terrorist attacks and homicides were less common when countries had high levels of globalization. Countries with high inequality and high urban percentage were significant for predicting homicide but had no significant effect on the frequency of terrorist attacks. Only the measure of poverty had no significant connection to either terrorist attacks or homicides.

A major difference between terrorism and more ordinary forms of crime emphasized throughout this Element is that the latter is far more common than the former. In a typical year, the United States will experience millions of felonies and thousands of murders but only a handful of terrorist attacks. Most countries of the world will not experience a single terrorist attack in a year. While the UNODC (2019) estimates that there were 277,994 homicides worldwide in 2017, GTD shows that there were a total of 26,892 terrorism-related fatalities the same year. Despite the enormous attention that terrorist attacks receive, they are far less common than other types of crime, including homicide.

Part of the challenge of integrating terrorism studies into mainstream criminology is that the integration is messy: terrorism resembles crime in some ways but also demonstrates important differences. Like ordinary crime, terrorism embodies a natural division between criminal etiology and law enforcement and requires an interdisciplinary emphasis. However, terrorist perpetrators, unlike more common criminal offenders, typically do not see themselves as criminals, are often seeking media attention and typically view their actions as furthering broader goals. Moreover, the study of terrorism lacks the main sources of traditional data that are available in criminology, and unlike most common crimes, terrorism frequently has national or even international implications.

The movement of mainstream criminology toward terrorism studies gathered a good deal of momentum after the coordinated attacks of 9/11 – barely two decades ago. However, the nature of perceived terrorist threats in the United States has greatly changed during the four presidential administrations since 9/11. In the immediate aftermath of the 9/11 attacks, the Bush administration focused its counterterrorism policies almost entirely on al Qaeda and the threats posed by the Salafist branch of Sunni Islam. President Bush introduced the term "violent extremism" in a policy statement in the summer of 2005 under the acronym SAVE (Struggle Against Violent Extremism), but treated it as one aspect of the global war on terror rather than a new domestic terrorism initiative (Schmitt & Shanker, 2005). In an address to a joint session of Congress, Bush (2004) made it clear that he regarded terrorism as a military rather than a criminal justice issue: "the fight against terrorism was not "primarily a law enforcement and intelligence gathering operation" but a "threat that demands the full use of American power."

The Obama administration took a more active interest in using criminal justice responses to counterterrorism. In a speech at Cairo University in Egypt shortly after his election, President Obama (2009) stated that his administration would place less emphasis on countering terrorism through military engagement and would instead shift more toward preventing the growth of violent extremism at home; although, Obama did not abandon military means for responding to international terrorism. For example, compared to the Bush administration, the Obama administration deployed even more drones for decapitation strikes. However, Obama emphasized much more strongly than Bush the importance of countering domestic extremism and a reliance on criminal justice over military approaches. The signature event in this shift was the 2015 Countering Violent Extremism Summit in which President Obama convened local and global leaders in Washington, DC, to present approaches to preventing violent extremism (White House, 2015). Counterterrorism approaches at this summit included not only military strategies but also policy recommendations from public health and gang prevention experts as well as local community activists.

Following his election, President Trump strongly signaled a move away from concerns with domestic terrorism (Ainsley, 2017) and back to a focus on countering terrorism through military strategies. Early in his administration, Trump unveiled a budget proposal that cut all funding to Department of Homeland Security countering domestic terrorism programs, which had previously provided grants to communities to counter radicalization through outreach (Congress eventually voted to continue funding the domestic programs). The move of the Trump administration toward an emphasis on prioritizing the fight against Islamist extremism over domestic extremist threats remained even after 2015 when the Islamic State lost most of the territory that it had claimed during earlier fighting. For many, Trump's lack of concern for right-wing domestic terrorism was demonstrated by his response to the Unite the Right rally in Charlottesville, North Carolina, in August 2017, which resulted in the death of one person and the injury of several dozen others. When he commented on the incident, Trump did not specifically denounce White nationalists, instead generally condemning "hatred, bigotry, and violence on many sides," and also noting that there were "very fine people on both sides" (Gray, 2017).

The divide between a focus on international and domestic terrorism reached a dramatic climax with the election of Joe Biden and the subsequent attack on the US Capitol on January 6, 2021. Supporters of Trump, intent on overturning his defeat in the 2020 presidential election, stormed the Capitol, breaching multiple police perimeters, and occupying, ransacking and vandalizing parts of the building (Dozier & Bergengruen, 2021; *Washington Post*, 2021). Trump was impeached on January 13, 2021 for inciting the January 6 attack on the US Capitol; however, he was acquitted in a Senate trial on February 13, 2021. On his first full day in office, President Biden directed his national security team to lead a 100-day comprehensive review of US government efforts to address domestic terrorism, and later released a national strategy for countering domestic terrorism.

Over the two decades spanning the Bush to the Biden administrations, criminology has played an important role in creating a social science aimed at understanding the causes and consequences of terrorism. Criminology should continue to play a major role in providing etiological theories and research methods for understanding terrorism and in establishing best practices for the processing of those accused of terrorism. Criminology has also benefitted by the broader interdisciplinary and comparative issues raised by the study of terrorism. Like white-collar and organized crime, terrorism has much in common with ordinary types of crime but also has major differences. Criminal justice investigations are indispensable for bringing those who use terrorist methods to justice. Compared to military approaches, criminal justice approaches are more limited and specific, longer term and less likely to produce collateral damage or threaten civil liberties. In the end, we should take more seriously Osama bin Laden's admission: "let history be a witness that I am a criminal" (Rahimullah, 1999).

References

Abadie, A. (2006). Poverty, political freedom, and the roots of terrorism. *American Economic Review*, 96(2), 50–56.

Abdo, G. (2006, August 27). America's Muslims aren't as assimilated as you think. *Washington Post*.

Aebi, M. F. (2010). Methodological issues in the comparison of police-recorded crime rates. In S. G. Shoham, P. Knepper & M. Kett (eds.), *International handbook of criminology* (pp. 211–227). CRC Press.

Ainsley, J. E. (2017, May 23). White House budget slashes "countering violent extremism" grants. *Reuters*.

Altier, M. B., Leonard Boyle, E., & Horgan, J. G. (2021). Returning to the fight: an empirical analysis of terrorist reengagement and recidivism. *Terrorism and Political Violence*, 33(4), 836–860.

Ancel, M. (1953). Le procès pénal et l'examen scientifique des délinquants. *Revue Internationale de Droit Comparé Année*, 5(2), 425-427.

Anderson, E. (1999). *Code of the street: decency, violence, and the moral life of the inner city*. W. W. Norton & Company.

Anselin, L. (1995). Local indicators of spatial association LISA. *Geographical Analysis*, 27, 93–115.

Argomaniz, J., & Vidal-Diez, A. (2015). Examining deterrence and backlash effects in counter-terrorism: the case of ETA. *Terrorism and Political Violence*, 27(1), 160–181.

Arnold, T. E., & Kennedy, M. (1988). *Think about terrorism: the new warfare*. Walker.

Arrigo, B. A. (2010). Identity, international terrorism and negotiating peace: Hamas and ethics-based considerations from critical restorative justice. *British Journal of Criminology*, 50(4), 772–790.

Avison, W. R., & Loring, P. L. (1986). Population diversity and cross-national homicide: the effects of inequality and heterogeneity. *Criminology*, 24(4), 733–749.

Bakker, E. (2006). *Jihadi terrorists in Europe, their characteristics and the circumstances in which they joined the jihad: an exploratory study*. Clingendael Institute.

Bankes, S. C. (2002). Agent-based modeling: a revolution? *Proceedings of the National Academy of Sciences*, 99(suppl. 3), 7199–7200.

Basuchoudhary, A., & Shughart, W. F. (2010). On ethnic conflict and the origins of transnational terrorism. *Defence and Peace Economics*, 21(1), 65–87.

Baumer, E. P., & Wolff, K. T. (2014). Evaluating contemporary crime drop(s) in America, New York City, and many other places. *Justice Quarterly*, 31(1), 5–38.

Becker, M. H., Decker, S. H., LaFree, G., et al. (2022). A comparative study of initial involvement in gangs and political extremism. *Terrorism and Political Violence*, 34(8), 1647–1664.

Behlendorf, B., LaFree, G., & Legault, R. (2012). Microcycles of Violence: evidence from terrorist attacks by ETA and the FMLN. *Journal of Quantitative Criminology*, 28(1), 49–75.

Bell, M. C. (2017). Police reform and the dismantling of legal cynicism. *Yale Law Journal*, 126, 2054–2150.

Bennett, R. (1991). Development and crime: a cross-national, time series analysis of competing models. *Sociological Quarterly*, 32(3), 343–363.

Berrebi, C. (2007). Evidence about the link between education, poverty and terrorism among Palestinians. *Peace Economics, Peace Science and Public Policy*, 13, 1–36.

Bersani, B. E., & Doherty, E. E. (2013). When the ties that bind unwind: examining the enduring and situational processes of change behind the marriage effect. *Criminology*, 51, 399–433.

Bjelopera, J. P. (2013, January 17). The domestic terrorist threat: background and issues for Congress. Congressional Research Service Report for Congress Prepared for Members and Committees of Congress.

Black, D. (1998). *The social structure of right and wrong*. Academic Press.

Blomberg, S. B., & Hess, G. D. (2006). How much does violence tax trade? *The Review of Economics and Statistics*, 88(4), 599–612.

Bloom, M. (2012). *Bombshell: women and terrorism*. University of Pennsylvania Press.

(2017). Women and terrorism. In *Oxford research encyclopedia of politics*. https://doi.org/10.1093/acrefore/9780190228637.013.124.

Borum, R. (2017). The etiology of radicalization. In G. LaFree & J. Freilich (eds.), *Handbook of the criminology of terrorism* (pp. 17–32). Wiley Blackwell.

Bouffard, L. A. (2003). Examining the relationship between military service and criminal behavior during the Vietnam era: a research note. *Criminology*, 41, 491–510.

Bouffard, L. A., & Laub, J. H. (2004). Jail or the army: does military service facilitate desistance from crime? In S. Maruna & Immarigeon, R. (eds.), *After crime and punishment: pathways to offender reintegration* (pp. 129–151). Willan.

Bove, V., & Böhmelt, T. (2016). Does immigration induce terrorism? *Journal of Politics*, 78(2), 572–588.

Bowers, K. J., & Johnson, S. D. (2004). Who commits near repeats? A test of the boost explanation. *Western Criminology Review*, 5(3), 12–24.

Bowie, N. G. (2017). Terrorism events data: an inventory of databases and data sets, 1968–2017. *Perspectives on Terrorism*, 11(4), 50–72.

Braithwaite, A., & Johnson, S. D. (2012). Space-time modeling of insurgency and counterinsurgency in Iraq. *Journal of Quantitative Criminology*, 28(1), 31–48.

Brockhoff, S., Krieger, T., & Meierrieks, D. (2015). Great expectations and hard times: the (nontrivial) impact of education on domestic terrorism. *Journal of Conflict Resolution*, 59(7), 1186–1215.

Bureau of Justice Statistics. (2022). *National crime victimization survey*. Bureau of Justice Statistics.

Bursik, R. J. (1988). Social disorganization and theories of crime and delinquency: problems and prospects. *Criminology*, 26(4), 519–552.

Bush, G. W. (2001). Address to a joint session of Congress and the American people.

(2004). President's remarks at victory 2004 rally in Hobbs, New Mexico, Oct. 11. White House Archives.

Campion, H. (1949). International statistics. *Journal of the Royal Statistical Society*, 112(2), 105–143.

Campos, N. F., & Gassebner, M. (2013). International terrorism, domestic political instability, and the escalation effect. *Economics & Politics*, 25(1), 27–47.

Carlsson, C., Rostami, A., Mondani, H., et al. (2020). A life-course analysis of engagement in violent extremist groups. *British Journal of Criminology*, 60(1), 74–92.

Carson, J. V. (2014). Counterterrorism and radical eco-groups: a context for exploring the series hazard model. *Journal of Quantitative Criminology*, 30(3), 485–504.

Carson, J. V., Dugan, L., & Yang, S.-M. (2020). A comprehensive application of rational choice theory: how costs imposed by, and benefits derived from, the US federal government affect incidents perpetrated by the radical eco-movement. *Journal of Quantitative Criminology*, 36(3), 701–724.

Caruso, R., & Schneider, F. (2011). The socio-economic determinants of terrorism and political violence in Western Europe (1994–2007). *European Journal of Political Economy*, 27, S37–S49.

Chenoweth, E. (2013). Terrorism and democracy. *Annual Review of Political Science*, 16, 355–378.

Choi, S. W, & Piazza, J. A (2016). Internally displaced populations and suicide terrorism. *Journal of Conflict Resolution*, 60(6), 1008–1040.

Choi, S. W. (2015). Economic growth and terrorism: domestic, international, and suicide. *Oxford Economic Papers*, 67(1), 157–181.

Choi, S. W., & Salehyan, I. (2013). No good deed goes unpunished: refugees, humanitarian aid, and terrorism. *Conflict Management and Peace Science*, 30(1), 53–75.

Clarke, R. V. (1980). Situational crime prevention: theory and practice. *British Journal of Criminology*, 20(2), 136–147.

(1995). Situational crime prevention. *Crime and Justice*, 19, 91–150.

(ed.). (1997). *Situational crime prevention: successful case studies* (2nd ed.). Harrow and Heston.

(2016). Situational crime prevention. In R. Wortley & M. Townsley (eds.), *Environmental criminology and crime analysis* (2nd ed., pp. 286–303). Routledge.

Clarke, R. V., & Cornish, D. B. (1985). Modeling offenders' decisions: a framework for research and policy. *Crime and Justice*, 6, 147–185.

Clarke, R. V., & Homel, R. (1997). A revised classification of situational crime prevention techniques. In S. P. Lab (ed.), *Crime prevention at a crossroads*. Academy of Criminal Justice Sciences.

Clarke, R. V., &, Newman, G. R. (2006). *Outsmarting the terrorists*. Praeger Security International.

Coccia, M. (2018). The relation between terrorism and high population growth. *Journal of Economics and Political Economy*, 5(1), 84–104.

Cohen, J., & Tita, G. (1999). Diffusion in homicide: exploring a general method for detecting spatial diffusion processes. *Journal of Quantitative Criminology*, 15(4), 451–493.

Cohen, L. E., & Felson, M. (1979). Social change and crime rate trends: a routine activity approach. *American Sociological Review*, 44, 588–608.

Cooley, J. K. (2002). *Unholy wars: Afghanistan, America and international terrorism*. Pluto Press.

Corner, E., & Gill, P. (2020). Psychological distress, terrorist involvement and disengagement from terrorism: a sequence analysis approach. *Journal of Quantitative Criminology*, (3)36, 499–526.

Cottee, S. (2020). The Western Jihadi subculture and subterranean values. *British Journal of Criminology*, 60(3), 762–781.

Cox, D. (1972). Regression models and life-tables. *Journal of the Royal Statistical Society*, 34, 187–220.

Crenshaw, M. (1983). *Terrorism, legitimacy, and power*. Wesleyan University Press.

Culver, L. (2004). The impact of new immigration patterns on the provision of police services in midwestern communities. *Journal of Criminal Justice*, 32(4), 329–344.

Dahl, E. (2011). The plots that failed: intelligence lessons learned from unsuccessful terrorist attacks against the United States. *Studies in Conflict and Terrorism*, 34(8), 621–648.

Danzell, O. E., & Zidek, S. (2013). Does counterterrorism spending reduce the incidence and lethality of terrorism? A quantitative analysis of 34 countries. *Defense and Security Analysis*, 29(3), 218–233.

Decker, S. H., Pyrooz, D. C., and Moule Jr., R. K. (2014). Disengagement from gangs as role transitions. *Journal of Research on Adolescence*, 24(2), 268–283.

DeLisi, M., Neppl, T. K., Lohman, B. J., Vaughn, M. G., & Shook, J. J. (2013). Early starters: which type of criminal onset matters most for delinquent careers? *Journal of Criminal Justice*, 41(1), 12–17.

Department of Homeland Security, Office of Intelligence and Analysis. (2009). *Rightwing extremism: current economic and political climate fueling resurgence in radicalization and recruitment*. United States Government.

Disha, I., Cavendish, J. C., & King, R. D. (2011). Historical events and spaces of hate: hate crimes against Arabs and Muslims in post-9/11 America. *Social Problems*, 58(1), 21–46.

Dozier, K., & Bergengruen, V. (2021, January 7). Incited by the President, pro-Trump rioters violently storm the Capitol. *TIME Magazine*. https://time .com/5926883/trump-supporters-storm-capitol/.

Dražanová, L. (2019). *The Austrian parliamentary elections 2019: are Austrians anti-immigrant?* European University Institute.

Dugan, L. (2011). The series hazard model: an alternative to time series for event data. *Journal of Quantitative Criminology*, 27, 379–402.

Dugan, L., LaFree, G., & Piquero, A. R. (2005). Testing a rational choice model of airline hijackings. *Criminology*, 43(4), 1031–1066.

Egger, C., & Magni-Berton, R. (2019). The role of Islamist ideology in shaping Muslim believers' attitudes toward terrorism: evidence from Europe. *Studies in Conflict & Terrorism*, 21(7), 1–24.

Eisner, M. (2008). Modernity strikes back? A historical perspective on the latest increase in interpersonal violence (1960–1990). *International Journal of Conflict and Violence*, 2(2), 288–316.

Enders, W., & Hoover, G. A. (2012). The nonlinear relationship between terrorism and poverty. *American Economic Review*, 102(3), 267–272.

Enders, W., Sandler, T., & Gaibulloev, K. (2011). Domestic versus transnational terrorism: data, decomposition, and dynamics. *Journal of Peace Research*, 48(3), 319–337.

Esty, D. C., Goldstone, J. A., Gurr, T. R., Surko, P., & Unger, A. N. (1995). *State failure task force report*. Science Applications International Corporation.

Eubank, W., & Weinberg, L. (2001). Terrorism and democracy: perpetrators and victims. *Terrorism and Political Violence*, 13(1), 155–164.

Ezcurra, R., & Palacios, D. (2016). Terrorism and spatial disparities: does interregional inequality matter? *European Journal of Political Economy*, 42(7), 60–74.

Fahey, S., & LaFree, G. (2015). Does country-level social disorganization increase terrorist attacks? *Terrorism and Political Violence*, 27(1), 81–111.

Fahey, S., LaFree, G., Dugan, L., & Piquero, A. R. (2012). A situational model for distinguishing terrorist and non-terrorist aerial hijackings, 1948–2007. *Justice Quarterly*, 29(4), 573–595.

Farrington, D. P. (2003). Developmental and life-course criminology: key theoretical and empirical issues – the 2002 Sutherland Award Address. *Criminology*, 41(2), 221–225.

Farrington, D., Ohlin, L., & Wilson, J.Q. (1986). *Understanding and controlling crime: toward a new research strategy*. Springer-Verlag.

Federal Bureau of Investigation (FBI). (2001a). *Crime in the United States 2001*. Uniform Crime Reports. US Government Printing Office.

(2001b). *Crime in the United States 2001*. Crimes in te United States Section V – Special Report. (pp. 301–314). US Government Printing Office. https://ucr.fbi.gov/crime-in-the-u.s/2001/01sec5.pdf.

(2008). *White supremacist recruitment of military personnel since 9/11*. US Government Printing Office.

(2017). *What is violent extremism?* US Federal Bureau of Investigation. https://cve.fbi.gov/whatis.

(2020). *Crime in the United States 2019*. Uniform Crime Reports. US Government Printing Office.

(2021). Strategic Intelligence Assessment and Data on Domestic Terrorism.

Feenstra, R. C., Inklaar, R., & Timmer, M. P. (2015). The next generation of the Penn World Table. *American Economic Review*, 105(10), 3150–3182. www.ggdc.net/pwt.

Forrester, A. C., Powell, B., Nowrasteh, A., & Landgrave, M. (2019). Do immigrants import terrorism? *Journal of Economic Behavior & Organization*, 166, 529–543.

Foster, D. M., Braithwaite, A., & Sobek, D. (2013). There can be no compromise: institutional inclusiveness, fractionalization and domestic terrorism. *British Journal of Political Science*, 43(3), 541–717.

Freilich, J. D., Adamczyk, A., Chermak, S. M., Boyd, K. A., & Parkin, W. S. (2015). Investigating the applicability of macro-level criminology theory to terrorism: A county-level analysis. *Journal of Quantitative Criminology*, 31(3), 383–411.

Freilich, J. D., Chermak, S. M., Belli, R., Gruenewald, J., & Parkin, W. S. (2014). Introducing the United States extremis crime database (ECDB). *Terrorism and Political Violence*, 26(2), 372–384.

Freilich, J. D, & LaFree, G. (2015). Criminology theory and terrorism. *Terrorism and Political Violence*, 27(1), 1–8.

Freytag, A., Krüger, J. J., Meierrieks, D., & Schneider, F. (2011). The origins of terrorism: cross-country estimates of socio-economic determinants of terrorism. *European Journal of Political Economy*, 27, S5–S16.

Gaibulloev, K., Piazza, J. A., & Sandler, T. (2017). Regime types and terrorism. *International Organization*, 71(3), 491–522.

Gendreau, P., Little, T., & Goggin, C. (1996). A meta-analysis of the predictors of adult offender recidivism: what works! *Criminology*, 34(4), 575–608.

Gill, P., Horgan, J., & Deckert, P. (2014). Bombing alone: tracing the motivations and antecedent behaviors of lone-actor terrorists. *Journal of Forensic Sciences*, 59(2), 425–435.

Glaser, D. (1964). *The effectiveness of a prison and parole system*. Bobbs-Merrill.

Gottfredson, D. (1997). School-based crime prevention. In *Preventing crime: what works, what doesn't, what's promising: a report to the United States Congress* (pp. 224–249). National Institute of Justice.

Gray, R. (2017, August 15). Trump defends white-nationalist protesters: "Some very fine people on both sides." *The Atlantic*.

Greene, Jack R., & Herzog, S. (2009). The implications of terrorism on the formal and social organization of policing in the United States and Israel: some concerns and opportunities. In D. L. Weisburd, T. E. Feucht, I. Hakimi, L. F. Mock & S. Perry (eds.), *To protect and to serve: policing in an age of terrorism* (pp. 143–176). Springer.

Gries, T., Krieger, T., & Meierrieks, D. (2011). Causal linkages between domestic terrorism and economic growth. *Defence and Peace Economics*, 22(5), 493–508.

Grogger, J. (1998). Market wages and youth crime. *Journal of Labor Economics*, 16(4), 756–791.

Groves, W. B., McCleary, R., & Newman, G. R. (1985). Religion, modernization, and world crime. *Comparative Social Research*, 8(1), 59–78.

Hafez, M. (2006). Rationality, culture, and structure in the making of suicide bombers: a preliminary theoretical synthesis and illustrative case study. *Studies in Conflict and Terrorism*, 29(2), 165–185.

(2008). Radicalization in the Persian Gulf: assessing the potential of Islamist militancy in Saudi Arabia and Yemen. *Dynamics of Asymmetric Conflict*, 1(1), 6–24.

Hamm, M. S. (1998). Terrorism, hate crime, and antigovernment violence: a review of the research. In H. W. Kushner (ed.), *The Future of Terrorism: Violence in the New Millennium* (pp.59–96). SAGE Publications.

(2007). *Terrorism as crime: from Oklahoma City to Al-Qaeda and beyond.* New York University Press.

(2009). Prison Islam in the age of sacred terror. *British Journal of Criminology*, 49(5), 667–685.

Hansmann, H. B., & Quigley, J. M. (1982). Population heterogeneity and the sociogenesis of homicide. *Social Forces*, 61(1), 206–224.

Hasisi, B., Carmel, T., & Wolfowicz, M. (2020a). Crime and terror: examining criminal risk factors for terrorist recidivism. *Journal of Quantitative Criminology*, 36(3), 449–472.

Hasisi, B., Perry, S., Ilan, Y., & Wolfowicz, M. (2020b). Concentrated and close to home: the spatial clustering and distance decay of lone terrorist vehicular attacks. *Journal of Quantitative Criminology*, 36(3), 607–645.

Hawkes, A. G. (1971). Spectra of some self-exciting and mutually exciting point processes. *Biometrika*, 58(1), 83–90.

Hewitt, C. (2003). *Understanding terrorism in America: from the Klan to al Qaeda*. Routledge.

Hill, R., Hubal, R., & Gowen, C. (2010). *Cooperation of immigrant communities to avert disaster: refined and improving focus on community strategy.* Institute for Homeland Security Solutions.

Hindelang, M. J., Hirschi, T., & Weis, J. G. (1979). Correlates of delinquency: the illusion of discrepancy between self-report and official measures. *American Sociological Review*, 44(6), 995–1014.

Hirschi, T. (1969). *Causes of delinquency.* University of California Press.

Hoffman, B. (1998). *Inside terrorism.* Columbia University Press.

Horgan, J. G. (2004). *The psychology of terrorism.* Routledge.

(2009). *Walking away from terrorism: accounts of disengagement from radical and extremist movements.* Routledge.

Howard, P. (2004). *Hard won lessons: how police fight terrorism in the United Kingdom.* Manhattan Institute for Policy Research.

Hsu, H. Y., & McDowall, D. (2020). Examining the state repression-terrorism nexus: dynamic relationships among repressive counterterrorism actions, terrorist targets, and deadly terrorist violence in Israel. *Criminology & Public Policy*, 19(2), 483–514.

Huizinga, D., & Elliott, D. S. (1986). Reassessing the reliability and validity of self-report delinquency measures. *Journal of Quantitative Criminology*, 2(4), 293–327.

Ilan, J., & Sandberg, S. (2019). How "gangsters" become jihadists: Bourdieu, criminology and the crime–terrorism nexus. *European Journal of Criminology*, 16(3), 278–294.

Jaggers, K., & Gurr, T. R. (1995). Tracking democracy's third wave with the Polity III data. *Journal of Peace Research*, 32(4), 469–482.

James, X., Hawkins, A., & Rowel, R. (2007). An assessment of the cultural appropriateness of emergency preparedness communication for low income minorities. *Journal of Homeland Security and Emergency Management*, 4(3), 1–26.

Jenkins, B. M. (1975). *Will terrorists go nuclear?* RAND Corporation.

Juergensmeyer, M. (2003). *Terror in the mind of God: the global rise of religious violence*. University of California Press.

Kamprad, A., & Liem, M. (2021). Terror and the legitimation of violence: a cross-national analysis on the relationship between terrorism and homicide rates. *Terrorism and Political Violence*, 33(1), 96–118.

Kanis, S., Messner, S. F., Eisner, M. P., & Heitmeyer, W. (2017). A cautionary note about the use of estimated homicide data for cross-national research. *Homicide Studies*, 21(4), 312–324.

Katz, J. (1988). *Seductions of crime: moral and sensual attractions in doing evil*. Basic Books.

Khashu, A., Busch, R., Latif, Z., & Levy, F. (2005). *Building strong police-immigrant community relations: lessons from a New York City project*. Vera Institute of Justice. Community Oriented Policing Services: US Department of Justice.

Kirk, D. S. (2012). Residential change as a turning point in the life course of crime: desistance or temporary cessation? *Criminology*, 50(2), 329–358.

Klausen, J., Morrill, T., & Libretti, R. (2016). The terrorist age-crime curve: an analysis of American Islamist terrorist offenders and age-specific propensity for participation in violent and nonviolent incidents. *Social Science Quarterly*, 97(1), 19–32.

Knox, G. (1964). Epidemiology of childhood leukemia in Northumberland and Durham. *British Journal of Prevention and Social Medicine*, 18, 17–24.

Krahn, H., Hartnagel, T. F., & Gartrell, J. W. (1986). Income inequality and homicide rates: cross-national data and criminological theories. *Criminology*, 24(2), 269–294.

Krieger, T., & Meierrieks, D. (2012). Does income inequality lead to terrorism? *SSRN Electronic Journal*. 2766910.

(2019). Income inequality, redistribution and domestic terrorism. *World Development*, 116, 125–136.

Krueger, A. B. (2007). *What makes a terrorist: economics and the roots of terrorism*. Princeton University Press.

Krueger, A. B., & Laitin, D. D. (2004a). Misunderestimating terrorism – the State Department's big mistake. *Foreign Affairs*, 83, 8.

(2004b, May 17). Faulty terror report card. *Washington Post*, A21.

(2008). Kto kogo? A cross-country study of the origins and targets of terrorism. *Terrorism, Economic Development, and Political Openness*, 5, 148–173.

Krueger, A. B., & Malečková, J. (2003). Education, poverty and terrorism: is there a causal connection? *Journal of Economic Perspectives*, 17(4), 119–144.

Kurrild-Klitgaard, P., Justesen, M. K., & Klemmensen, R. (2006). The political economy of freedom, democracy and transnational terrorism. *Public Choice*, 128(1–2), 289–315.

LaFree, G. (1999). A summary and review of cross-national comparative studies of homicide. In M. D. Smith & M. A. Zahn (eds.), *Homicide: a sourcebook of social research*.(pp. 125-148). Sage.

(2022). Terrorism open-source databases. In D. Muro & T. Wilson (eds.), *Contemporary Terrorism Studies* (pp. 113–134). Oxford University Press.

LaFree, G., & Ackerman, G. (2009). The empirical study of terrorism: social and legal research. *Annual Review of Law and Social Science*, 5, 347–374.

LaFree, G., & Bersani, B. E. (2014). County-level correlates of terrorist attacks in the United States. *Criminology & Public Policy*, 13(3), 455–481.

LaFree, G., & Dugan, L. (2004). How does studying terrorism compare to studying crime. *Terrorism and Counter-terrorism: Criminological Perspectives*, 5, 53–74.

(2007). Introducing the Global Terrorism Database. *Terrorism and Political Violence*, 19(2), 181–204.

LaFree, G., Dugan, L., & Fahey, S. (2008). Global terrorism and failed states. In *Peace and Conflict 2008* (pp. 39–54). Paradigm.

LaFree, G., Dugan, L., & Korte, R. (2009). The impact of British counter terrorist strategies on political violence in Northern Ireland: comparing deterrence and backlash models. *Criminology*, 47(1), 501–530.

LaFree, G., Dugan, L., & Miller, E. (2015). *Putting terrorism in context: lessons from the global terrorism database*. Routledge.

LaFree, G., Dugan, L., Xie, M., & Singh, P. (2012). Spatial and temporal patterns of terrorist attacks by ETA 1970 to 2007. *Journal of Quantitative Criminology*, 28(1), 7–29.

LaFree, G., & Freilich, J. (2012). Editor's introduction: quantitative approaches to the study of terrorism. *Journal of Quantitative Criminology*, 28, 1–5.

LaFree, G., Jensen, M. A., James, P. A., & Safer-Lichtenstein, A. (2018). Correlates of violent political extremism in the United States. *Criminology*, 56(2), 233–268.

LaFree, G., & Jiang, B. (2022). Globalization and cross-national homicide. Paper presented at the annual meetings of the European Society of Criminology, Malaga, Spain, September 22, 2022.

LaFree, G., Jiang, B., & Porter, L. (2020). Prison and violent political extremism in the United States. *Journal of Quantitative Criminology*, 36(3), 1–26.

LaFree, G., & Kick, E. L. (1986). Cross-national effects of developmental, distributional, and demographic variables on crime: a review and analysis. *International Annals of Criminology*, 24, 213–236.

LaFree, G., Morris, N. A., & Dugan, L. (2010). Cross-national patterns of terrorism: comparing trajectories for total, attributed and fatal attacks, 1970–2006. *British Journal of Criminology*, 50(4), 622–649.

LaFree, G., & Tseloni, A. (2006). Democracy and crime: a multilevel analysis of homicide trends in forty-four countries, 1950–2000. *The Annals of the American Academy of Political and Social Science*, 605(1), 25–49.

LaFree, G., Xie, M., & Matanock, A. M. (2018). The contagious diffusion of worldwide terrorism: is it less common than we might think? *Studies in Conflict and Terrorism*, 41(4), 261–280.

LaFree, G., & Yanez, Y. (in press). Criminological perspectives on extremist radicalization and mobilization. In J. Busher, L. Malkki & S. Marsden (eds.), *Handbook on radicalization and countering radicalization*. Routledge.

LaFree, G., Yang, S. M., & Crenshaw, M. (2009). Trajectories of terrorism: attack patterns of foreign groups that have targeted the United States, 1970 to 2004. *Criminology & Public Policy*, 8(3), 445–473.

Lappi-Seppälä, T., & Tonry, M. (2011). Crime, criminal justice, and criminology in the Nordic countries. *Crime and Justice*, 40(1), 1–32.

Levchak, P. J. (2015). Extending the anomie tradition: an assessment of the impact of trade measures on cross-national homicide rates. *Homicide Studies*, 19(4), 384–400.

Li, Q. (2005). Does democracy promote or reduce transnational terrorist incidents? *Journal of Conflict Resolution*, 49(2), 278–297.

Lipsey, M. W., & Wilson, D. B. (2001). *Practical meta-analysis*. SAGE Publications.

Lochner, L., & Moretti, E. (2004). The effect of education on crime: evidence from prison inmates, arrests, and self-reports. *American Economic Review*, 94(1), 155–189.

Lysova, A. (2020). Challenges to the veracity and the international comparability of Russian homicide statistics. *European Journal of Criminology*, 17(4), 399–419.

Marchment, Z., Gill, P., & Morrison, J. (2020). Risk factors for violent dissident republican incidents in Belfast: a comparison of bombings and bomb hoaxes. *Journal of Quantitative Criminology*, 36(3), 647–666.

Marsella, A. J., Johnson, J. L., Watson, P., & Gryczynski, J. (eds.). (2008). *Ethnocultural perspectives on disaster and trauma: foundations, issues, and applications*. Springer.

Masters, D., & Hoen, P. (2012). State legitimacy and terrorism. *Democracy and Security*, 8(4), 337–357.

McAlexander, R. J. (2020). How are immigration and terrorism related? An analysis of right-and left-wing terrorism in Western Europe, 1980–2004. *Journal of Global Security Studies*, 5(1), 179–195.

McCauley, C. (2002). Psychological issues in understanding terrorism and the response to terrorism. C. E. Stout (ed.), *The psychology of terrorism: theoretical understandings and perspectives, Vol. 3* (pp. 3–29). Praeger Publishers/Greenwood Publishing Group.

McCauley, C., & Moskalenko, S. (2008). Mechanisms of political radicalization: pathways toward terrorism. *Terrorism and Political Violence*, 20(3), 415–433.

McMillan, C., Felmlee, D., & Braines, D. (2020). Dynamic patterns of terrorist networks: efficiency and security in the evolution of eleven islamic extremist attack networks. *Journal of Quantitative Criminology*, 36(3), 559–581.

Mendelsohn, B. (2011). Foreign fighters – recent trends. *Orbis*, 55(2), 189–202.

Menjívar, C., & Bejarano, C. (2004). Latino immigrants' perceptions of crime and police authorities in the United States: a case study from the Phoenix metropolitan area. *Ethnic and Racial Studies*, 27(1), 120–148.

Merari, A. (1991). Academic research and government policy on terrorism. *Terrorism and Political Violence*, 3(1), 88–102.

Messner de Latour, J. J., Haken, N. Taft, P. et al. (2020). Fragile states index annual report 2020. https://fragilestatesindex.org/2020/05/08/fragile-states-index-2020-annual-report/.

Messner, S. F. (1982). Societal development, social equality, and homicide: a cross-national test of a Durkheimian model. *Social Forces*, 61(1), 225–240.

Messner, S. F., Raffalovich, L. E., & Sutton, G. M. (2010). Poverty, infant mortality, and homicide rates in cross-national perspective: assessments of criterion and construct validity. *Criminology*, 48(2), 509–537.

Mickolus, E. F. (1976). *International terrorism: attributes of terrorist events: ITERATE*. Inter-university Consortium for Political and Social Research.

(2002). How do we know we're winning the war against terrorists? Issues in measurement. *Studies in Conflict and Terrorism*, 25(3), 151–160. https://doi.org/10.1080/01490380290073158.

Mickolus, E. F., Sandler, T., Murdock, J. M., & Flemming, P. (2010). *International terrorism: attributes of terrorist events (ITERATE)*. Vinyard Software.

Miller, E. (2012). Patterns of onset and decline among terrorist organizations. *Journal of Quantitative Criminology*, 28(1), 77–101.

Miller, V., & Hayward, K. J. (2019). "I did my bit": terrorism, Tarde and the vehicle ramming attack as an imitative event. *British Journal of Criminology*, 59(1), 1–23.

Moghadam A. (2006). The roots of suicide terrorism: a multi-causal approach. In A. Pedhazur (ed.). *Root causes of suicide terrorism: the globalization of martyrdom* (pp. 81–107). Routledge.

Mohler, G. O. (2014). Marked point process hotspot maps for homicide and gun crime prediction in Chicago. *International Journal of Forecasting*, 30(3), 491–497.

Mohler, G. O., Short, M. B., Brantingham, P. J., Schoenberg, F. P., & Tita, G. E. (2011). Self-exciting point process modeling of crime. *Journal of the American Statistical Association*, 106(493), 100–108.

Morris, N. A., & LaFree, G. (2017). Country-level predictors of terrorism. In G. LaFree & J. Freilich (eds.), *Handbook of the criminology of terrorism* (pp. 93–117). Wiley Blackwell.

Morris, N. A., & Slocum, L. A. (2012). Estimating country-level terrorism trends using group-based trajectory analyses: latent class growth analysis and general mixture modeling. *Journal of Quantitative Criminology*, 28 (1), 103–139.

Mythen, G., & Walklate, S. (2006). Criminology and terrorism: which thesis? Risk society or governmentality? *British Journal of Criminology*, 46(3), 379–398.

Nagin, D. S., & Land, K. C. (1993). Age, criminal careers, and population heterogeneity: specification and estimation of a nonparametric, mixed Poisson model. *Criminology*, 31(3), 327–362.

Nagin, D. S., & Tremblay, R. E. (1999). Trajectories of boys' physical aggression, opposition, and hyperactivity on the path to physically violent and nonviolent juvenile delinquency. *Child Development*, 70(5), 1181–1196.

National Law Enforcement Memorial Fund. (2021). Law enforcement facts. https://nleomf.org/memorial/facts-figures/law-enforcement-facts/.

Nivette, A. E. (2011). Cross-national predictors of crime: a meta-analysis. *Homicide Studies*, 15(2), 103–131.

Nivette, A. E., Eisner, M., & Ribeaud, D. (2017). Developmental predictors of violent extremist attitudes: a test of general strain theory. *Journal of Research in Crime and Delinquency*, 54(6), 755–790.

Obama, B. (2009). President Obama speaks to the Muslim world from Cairo, Egypt. The White House: President Barack Obama. National Archives and Records Administration.

Ortbals, C. D., & Poloni-Staudinger, L. M. (2018). *Gender and political violence: women changing the politics of terrorism.* Springer.

Ortega, S. T., Corzine, J., Burnett, C., & Poyer, T. (1992). Modernization, age structure and regional context: a cross-national study of crime. *Sociological Spectrum*, 12(3), 257–277.

Ozaki, T. (1979). Maximum likelihood estimation of Hawkes' self-exciting point processes. *Annals of the Institute of Statistical Mathematics*, 31(1), 145–155.

Pape, R. A. (2005). *Dying to win: the strategic logic of suicide terrorism.* Random House.

Pape, R. A., Rivas, A. A., & Chinchilla, A. C. (2021). Introducing the new CPOST dataset on suicide attacks. *Journal of Peace Research*, 58(4), 826–838.

Pauwels, L. J., Ljujic, V., & de Buck, A. (2020). Individual differences in political aggression: the role of social integration, perceived grievances and low self-control. *European Journal of Criminology*, 17(5), 603–627.

Pedahzur, A., Perliger, A., & Weinberg, L., (2003). Altruism and fatalism: the characteristics of Palestinian suicide terrorists. *Deviant Behavior*, 24(4), 405–423.

Perry, S. (2020). The application of the "law of crime concentration" to terrorism: the Jerusalem case study. *Journal of Quantitative Criminology*, 36(3), 583–605.

Perry, S., Apel, R., Newman, G. R., & Clarke, R. V. (2017). The situational prevention of terrorism: an evaluation of the Israeli West Bank barrier. *Journal of Quantitative Criminology*, 33(4), 727–751.

Perry, S., & Hasisi, B. (2015). Rational choice rewards and the jihadist suicide bomber. *Terrorism and Political Violence*, 27(1), 53–80.

Piazza, J. A. (2008a). Do democracy and free markets protect us from terrorism? *International Politics*, 45(1), 72–91.

(2008b). Incubators of terror: do failed and failing states promote transnational terrorism? *International Studies Quarterly*, 52(3), 469–488.

(2011). Poverty, minority economic discrimination, and domestic terrorism. *Journal of Peace Research*, 48(3), 339–353.

(2012). Types of minority discrimination and terrorism. *Conflict Management and Peace Science*, 29(5), 521–546.

(2013). Regime age and terrorism: are new democracies prone to terrorism? *International Interactions*, 39(2), 246–263.

Piazza, J. A., & LaFree, G. (2019). Islamist terrorism, diaspora links and casualty rates. *Perspectives on Terrorism*, 13(5), 2–21.

Plümper, T., & Neumayer, E. (2010). Model specification in the analysis of spatial dependence. *European Journal of Political Research*, 49(3), 418–442.

Porter, M. D., & White, G. (2012). Self-exciting hurdle models for terrorist activity. *The Annals of Applied Statistics*, 6(1), 106–124.

Pratt, T. C., & Cullen, F. T. (2005). Assessing macro-level predictors and theories of crime: a meta-analysis. *Crime and Justice*, 32, 373–450.

Pridemore, W. A. (2008). A methodological addition to the crossnational empirical literature on social structure and homicide: a first test of the poverty-homicide thesis. *Criminology*, 46(1), 133–154.

Pyrooz, D., LaFree, G., Decker, S., & James, P. (2017). Cut from the same cloth? Comparing gangs and violent political extremists. *Justice Quarterly*, 35(1), 1–32.

Python, A., Brandsch, J., & Tskhay, A. (2017). Provoking local ethnic violence – a global study on ethnic polarization and terrorist targeting. *Political Geography*, 58, 77–89.

Quinney, R. (1965). Suicide, homicide, and economic development. *Social Forces*, 43(3), 401–406.

Rahimullah, Y. (1999, January 11). Conversation with terror. *TIME Magazine*.

Ranstorp, M. (2007). *Mapping terrorism research*. Routledge.

Rennó Santos, M., Testa, A., & Weiss, D. B. (2018). Where poverty matters: examining the cross-national relationship between economic deprivation and homicide. *British Journal of Criminology*, 58(2), 372–393.

Rogers, M. L., & Pridemore, W. A. (2023). A review and analysis of the impact of homicide measurement on cross-national research. *Annual Review of Criminology*, 6.

Rosenbaum, D. P., Schuck, A. M., Costello, S. K., Hawkins, D. F., & Ring, M. K. (2005). Attitudes toward the police: the effects of direct and vicarious experience. *Police Quarterly*, 8(3), 343–368.

Ruggiero, V. (2010). Armed struggle in Italy: the limits to criminology in the analysis of political violence. *British Journal of Criminology*, 50(4), 708–724.

Rummel, R. J. (1994). *Death by government*. Transaction Books.

Russell, C. A., & Miller, B. H. (1977). Profile of a terrorist. *Military Review*, 57, 21–34.

Sageman, M. (2004). *Understanding terror networks*. University of Pennsylvania Press.

(2008). *Leaderless Jihad: terror in the twenty-first century*. University of Pennsylvania Press.

(2014). The stagnation in terrorism research. *Terrorism and Political Violence*, 26(4), 565–580.

Savun, B., & Phillips, B. J. (2009). Democracy, foreign policy, and terrorism. *Journal of Conflict Resolution*, 53(6), 878–904.

Schmid, A. P., & Jongman, A. J. (1988). *Political terrorism: a new guide to actors, authors, concepts, databases, theories and literature*. North-Holland

Schmitt, E., & Shanker, T. (2005, July 26). US officials retool slogan for terror war. *New York Times*.

Schuurman, B. (2020). Research on terrorism, 2007–2016: a review of data, methods, and authorship. *Terrorism and Political Violence*, 32(5), 1011–1026.

Semmelbeck, J., & Besaw, C. (2020). Exploring the determinants of crime-terror cooperation using machine learning. *Journal of Quantitative Criminology*, 3(36), 527–558.

Shapiro, J. N. (2013). *The terrorist's dilemma: managing violent covert organizations*. Princeton University Press.

Sharvit, K., Kruglanski, A. W., Wang, M. et al. (2013). The effects of Israeli use of coercive and conciliatory tactics on Palestinian's use of terrorist tactics: 2000–2006. *Dynamics of Asymmetric Conflict*, 6(1–3), 22–44.

Shaw, C. R., & McKay, H. D. (1942). *Juvenile delinquency and urban areas*. University of Chicago Press.

Sherman, L. W., Gartin, P. R., & Buerger, M. E. (1989). Hot spots of predatory crime: routine activities and the criminology of place. *Criminology*, 27(1), 27–56.

Shichor, D. (1990). Crime patterns and socioeconomic development: a cross-national analysis. *Criminal Justice Review*, 15(1), 64–78.

Shiu-Thornton, S., Balabis, J., Senturia, K., Tamayo, A., & Oberle, M. (2007). Disaster preparedness for limited English proficient communities: medical interpreters as cultural brokers and gatekeepers. *Public Health Reports*, 122(4), 466–471.

Silke, A. (2001). The devil you know: continuing problems with research on terrorism. *Terrorism and Political Violence*, 13(4), 1–14.

(2008). Holy warriors: exploring the psychological processes of Jihadi radicalization. *European Journal of Criminology*, 5(1), 99–123.

Simi, P., Sporer, K., & Bubolz, B. (2016). Narratives of childhood adversity and adolescent misconduct as precursors to violent extremism: a lifecourse criminological approach. *Journal of Research in Crime and Delinquency*, 53(4), 536–563.

Simpson, G. (1933). *Emile Durkheim on the division of labor in society, being a translation of his* De la Division Du Travail Social, *with an estimate of his work*. Macmillan.

Simpson, M. (2014). Terrorism and corruption. *International Journal of Sociology*, 44(2), 87–104.

Sjoberg, L., & Gentry, C. E. (eds.) (2011). *Women, gender and terrorism*. University of Georgia Press.

Smit, P. R., de Jong, R. R., & Bijleveld, C. C. (2012). Homicide data in Europe: definitions, sources, and statistics. In *Handbook of European Homicide Research* (pp. 5–23). Springer.

Smith, B. L. (1994). *Terrorism in America: pipe bombs and pipe dreams*. State University of New York Press.

Smith, B. L., & Damphousse, K. R. (2007). American Terrorism Study, 1980–2002. Inter-university Consortium for Political and Social Research.

Smith, M. D., Devine, J. A., & Sheley, J. F. (1992). Crime and unemployment: effects across age and race categories. *Sociological Perspectives*, 35(4), 551–572.

Solt, F. (2016). The standardized world income inequality database. *Social Science Quarterly*, 97(5), 1267–1281.

Stern, J. (2002). Dreaded risks and the control of biological weapons. *International Security*, 27(3), 89–123.

Sturup, J., Gerell, M., & Rostami, A. (2020). Explosive violence: a near-repeat study of hand grenade detonations and shootings in urban Sweden. *European Journal of Criminology*, 17(5), 661–677.

Sumpter, C. (2017). Countering violent extremism in Indonesia: priorities, practice and the role of civil society. *Journal for Deradicalization*, (11), 112–147.

Sutherland, E. H., & Cressey, D. (1960) *Principles of criminology* (6th ed.). Lippencott.

Sweeten, G., Piquero, A. R., & Steinberg, L. (2013). Age and the explanation of crime, revisited. *Journal of Youth and Adolescence*, 42, 921–938.

Tauchen, H. V., Witte, A. D., & Griesinger, H. (1994). Criminal deterrence: revisiting the issue with a birth cohort. *The Review of Economics and Statistics*, 76(3), 399–412.

Townsley, M., Homel, R., & Chaseling, J. (2003). Infectious burglaries. A test of the near repeat hypothesis. *British Journal of Criminology*, 43(3), 615–633.

Townsley, M., Johnson, S. D., & Ratcliffe, J. H. (2008). Space time dynamics of insurgent activity in Iraq. *Security Journal*, 21(3), 139–146.

Turk, A. T. (1982). *Political criminality: The defiance and defense of authority.* SAGE Publications.

Tyler, T. R., Schulhofer, S., & Huq, A. Z. 2010. Legitimacy and deterrence effects in counterterrorism policing: a study of Muslim Americans. *Law and Society Review*, 44(2), 365–402.

Uggen, C. (2000). Work as a turning point in the life course of criminals: a duration model of age, employment, and recidivism. *American Sociological Review*, 65(4), 529–546.

UNODC. (2019). *Global study on homicide 2019.* UNODC.

Useem, B., & Clayton, O. (2009). Radicalization of U. S. prisoners. *Criminology and Public Policy*, 8(3), 561–92.

Varaine, S. (2020). Revisiting the economics and terrorism nexus: collective deprivation, ideology and domestic radicalization in the U. S. (1948–2016). *Journal of Quantitative Criminology*, 36, 667–699.

Vetere, E., & Newman, G. (1977). International crime statistics: an overview from a comparative perspective. *Abstracts on Criminology and Penology*, 17(3), 251–267.

Vigderhous, G., (1978). Methodological problems confronting cross-cultural criminological research using official data. *Human Relations*, 31(3), 229–247.

Washington Post (2021, January 7). Trump supporters storm Capitol; DC National Guard activated; woman fatally shot.

Weber, S. (2006). *Perceptions of the United States and support for violence against America.* Research brief. National Consortium for the Study of Terrorism and Response to Terrorism.

Weisburd, D., Wolfowicz, M., Hasisi, B., Paolucci, M., & Andrighetto, G. (2022). What is the best approach for preventing recruitment to terrorism? Findings from ABM experiments in social and situational prevention. *Criminology & Public Policy*, 21(2), 461–485.

White, G., Porter, M. D., & Mazerolle, L. (2013). Terrorism risk, resilience and volatility: a comparison of terrorism patterns in three Southeast Asian countries. *Journal of Quantitative Criminology*, 29(2), 295–320.

White House. (2015). *Fact sheet: the White House summit on countering violent extremism.* Press Secretary. White House Office.

Wigle, J. (2010). Introducing the Worldwide Incidents Tracking System (WITS). *Perspectives on Terrorism*, 4(1), 3–23.

Wilson, M. C., & Piazza, J. A. (2013). Autocracies and terrorism: conditioning effects of authoritarian regime type on terrorist attacks. *American Journal of Political Science*, 57(4), 941–955.

Witte, A. D., & Tauchen, H. (2000). *Work and crime: an exploration using panel data*. Palgrave Macmillan UK.

Wolf, P. (1971). Crime and development: an international comparison of crime rates. *Scandinavian Studies in Criminology*, 3, 107–120.

Wolfowicz, M., Litmanovitz, Y., Weisburd, D., & Hasisi, B. (2020). A field-wide systematic review and meta-analysis of putative risk and protective factors for radicalization outcomes. *Journal of Quantitative Criminology*, 36, 407–447.

World Bank Open Data. (2020). https://data.worldbank.org/.

Cambridge Elements ≡

Criminology

David Weisburd
George Mason University
Hebrew University of Jerusalem

Advisory Board
Professor Catrien Bijleveld, *VU University Amsterdam*
Professor Francis Cullen, *University of Cincinnati School of Criminal Justice*
Professor Manuel Eisner, *Cambridge University*
Professor Elizabeth Groff, *Temple University*
Professor Cynthia Lum, *George Mason University*
Professor Lorraine Mazerolle, *University of Queensland*
Professor Daniel Nagin, Teresa and H. John Heinz III, *Carnegie Mellon University*
Professor Ojmarrh Mitchell, *University of South Florida*
Professor Alex Piquero, Ashbel Smith, *University of Texas at Dallas*
Professor Richard Rosenfeld, *University of Missouri*

About the series
Elements in Criminology seeks to identify key contributions in theory and empirical research that help to identify, enable, and stake out advances in contemporary criminology. The series will focus on radical new ways of understanding and framing criminology, whether of place, communities, persons, or situations. The relevance of criminology for preventing and controlling crime will also be a key focus of this series.

Cambridge Elements ☰

Criminology

Elements in the Series

Developmental Criminology and the Crime Decline
Jason L. Payne, Alexis R. Piquero

A Framework for Addressing Violence and Serious Crime
Anthony A. Braga, David M. Kennedy

Whose 'Eyes on the Street' Control Crime?: Expanding Place Management into Neighborhoods
Shannon J. Linning, John E. Eck

Confronting School Violence: A Synthesis of Six Decades of Research
Jillian J. Turanovic, Travis C. Pratt, Teresa C. Kulig, Francis T. Cullen

Testing Criminal Career Theories in British and American Longitudinal Studies
John F. MacLeod, David P. Farrington

Legitimacy-Based Policing and the Promotion of Community Vitality
Tom Tyler, Caroline Nobo

Making Sense of Youth Crime: Intelligence Analysis in the American and French Police
Jacqueline E. Ross, Thierry Delpeuch

Toward a Criminology of Terrorism
Gary LaFree

A full series listing is available at: www.cambridge.org/ECRM

Printed in the United States
by Baker & Taylor Publisher Services